Karate Kata

For the Transmission
of High-Level
Combative
Skills

Vol. 1

An
Anthology
of Articles
from the
*Journal of
Asian Martial Arts*

Edited by Michael A. DeMarco, M.A.

Copyright © 2015 by
Via Media Publishing Company
941 Calle Mejia #822
Santa Fe, NM 87501 USA
E-mail: md@goviamedia.com

All articles in this anthology were originally published in the *Journal of Asian Martial Arts*. Listed according to the table of contents for this anthology:

Donohue, J. (2006)	Volume 15, Number 3	pages 8–19
Labbate, M. (1999)	Volume 8, Number 2	pages 80–95
Labbate, M. (2000)	Volume 9, Number 1	pages 56–69
Labbate, M. (2001)	Volume 10, Number 1	pages 84–99
Toth, R. (2001)	Volume 10, Number 3	pages 84–91
Labbate, M. (2002)	Volume 11, Number 1	pages 80–95
Hopkins, G. (2002)	Volume 11, Number 4	pages 54–77

Book and cover design by Via Media Publishing Company

Edited by Michael A. DeMarco, M.A.

ISBN: 978-1-893765-13-9

Cover illustration

Painting of Shihan Toshio Tamano courtesy of Feodor Tamarsky.
Copyright by F. Tamarsky. www.tamarskygallery.com

www.viamediapublishing.com

contents

iv   **Preface**
Michael DeMarco, M.A.

v   **Author Bio Notes**

CHAPTERS

1   Kaho: Cultural Meaning and Educational Method in Kata Training
by John Donohue, Ph.D.

14   Elements of Advanced Techniques
by Marvin Labbate

33   Developing Advanced Goju-Ryu Techniques
by Marvin Labbate

52   Tensho Kata: Goju-Ryu's Secret Treasure
by Marvin Labbate

70   An Analysis of Parallel Techniques:
The Kinetic Connection Between Sanseru and Shishochin
by Robert Toth

79   Incorporating the Main Principles of Kata Training
by Marvin Labbate

97   The Lost Secrets of Okinawan Goju-Ryu: What the Kata Shows
by Giles Hopkins, M.A.

121   **Index**

preface

We all know the meaning of the word kata. Even to nonpractitioners it is a familiar karate practice. Plus, the word has long been incorporated into the English language. For this reason I choose to write the plural as "katas," and not follow the Japanese tradition where "kata" can be both singular or plural. By doing this I've ruffled feathers already, since many hold such a sacred bond with the time and place where karate took shape. Trouble with one word? Now how about the whole Okinawan martial tradition as passed on through katas?

A kata is much like a family jewel that has passed down through generations. It holds a significance that is difficult to decipher, and many dispute the meaning of every micromovement it contains. Who created it? What are the applications? Is kata practice outdated? Is there more than we can see and understand? You bet.

It is precisely because of the confusion and misunderstandings regarding the place of kata in the karate tradition that we are thrilled to present a two-volume e-book on this subject. If katas are learning tools that pass down knowledge of a valued art, then the authors included in this anthology can certainly facilitate the learning process for all interested in karate. Each author has excellent experience in the field, having studied directly under masters, often on the largest island in the Ryukyu island chain. In addition to their long years of physical participation in the school of hard knocks, their depth of scholarly research into the encompassing culture allows their writings to illuminate many aspects of kata practice that normally go unnoticed.

In our quest to better understand the full significance of kata practice, we must take a serious look at why old masters formulated the routines. How can kata practice better our health and promise to hone our self-defense skills? Each chapter in this anthology deals with the principles that guide kata practice. Hopefully the reading will reveal some of the secrets to improving techniques. As with other martial traditions, some insights cannot be shared through written word. Like good teachers, may the chapters here inspire you to look deeper into kata practice.

Michael A. DeMarco
Santa Fe
September 2015

author bio notes

John J. Donohue, Ph.D., a longtime practitioner of Japanese martial arts, Dr. Donohue's professional background includes a Ph.D. in anthropology from the State University of New York at Stony Brook. In addition to academic articles and books dealing with martial culture, John is a novelist. His fictional works have a strong thread of martial culture woven into the themes. See www.johndonohue.net.

Giles Hopkins, M.A., a teacher of English and history, received a B.A. degree in English literature from the State University of New York and an M.A. degree in history from the University of Massachusetts at Amherst. He has been training in the martial arts since 1973 and holds sixth dan rankings and a teacher's certificate in Okinawan Goju-Ryu and Matayoshi kobudo. His teacher is Kimo Wall, seventh dan and president of Kodokan, in the lineage of Higa Seiko and Matayoshi Shinpo.

Mario McKenna, M.S., holds a master of science from the University of Saskatchewan, and master of health administration from the University of British Columbia. He began his training in Okinawa Goju-Ryu and Tomarite (Gohakukai) karatedo in 1984 under Kinjo Yoshitaka. From 1994 to 2002 he resided in Japan, where he studied Ryukyu kobudo from Minowa Katsuhiko and Yoshimura Hiroshi, and Tou'on-Ryu karatedo from Kanzaki Shigekazu. He is ranked third dan, Gohakukai; fifth dan, Ryukyu kobudo; and fifth dan, Tou'on-Ryu. He teaches in Vancouver, Canada.

Marvin Labbate is an eighth dan black belt in Okinawa Goju-Ryu, fifth dan in Okinawan Ryukonkai kobudo, and a certified Yang taijiquan instructor. He has studied karate for over thirty-five years and is the international representative for the Okinawan Seibukai Association under President Nakasone Kinei, tenth degree. Mr. Labbate is the director of CNY Karate (www.cnykarate.com), founded in 1963, which is the oldest karate school in upstate New York.

Robert Toth has been training in the martial arts for over thirty years. His sensei was the late Dr. Richard Kim, tenth dan. Bob received a teaching grade of fourth dan black belt from Dr. Kim. After Dr. Kim's passing, Bob became a student by Yagi Meitatsu, tenth dan, of Okinawa, Japan. He recently graded in Okinawa to fifth dan with Sensei Yagi and the International Meibukan Gojyu-Ryu Karate-Do Association. Sensei Toth is a published author of the martial arts, as well as an international teacher, lecturer, and tournament judge. Bob teaches at the St. Catharines Martial Arts Centre in Canada.

Kaho: Cultural Meaning and Educational Method in Kata Training

by John J. Donohue, Ph.D.

The trainee stands garbed in the robes of a by-gone era, gripping a weapon as deadly as it is archaic. The world tightens down to a small universe built of hard wood, polished steel, cotton cloth, body heat, sweat, and the tidal pulse of heart-beat and respiration. Here, the weapon is wielded in a sequence of moves set down by masters long gone, actions refined and repeated until the performer is lost in the hiss of effort and the focused pursuit of perfection. It is a curious thing, part technical exercise, part performance art, part meditative experience. It is kata.

Introduction

The world of the Asian martial arts is one that has gripped the imagination of Westerners for decades now. Its trappings strike the outside viewer as exotic, its motivations arcane. It is dense with symbolism and occluded meaning. It is rife with opportunity for misunderstanding and romanticization. It is, in short, a social phenomenon that cries out for anthropological analysis.

Students of many modern Japanese martial arts are fond of reminding us, as the Japanese term *budo* implies, that they are really "martial ways." The destination of these ways is varied: they can be understood as systems of physical exercise or spiritual development, as relatively efficient physiological (as opposed to technological) systems, as recreational and competitive sports, or as civilian self-defense methods. In fact, any intense scrutiny of these systems reveals a multifaceted nature in which aspects of all these things can be recognized. The deeper the understanding of budo, the greater their recognized complexity.

This sophistication relates not merely to the techniques and systems themselves, but to the way in which they have been taught within the Japanese martial tradition. This represents another avenue of scientific inquiry for researchers focusing on sociological interpretations of martial arts activity.

I will examine the structure and purpose of the practice patterns known in the Japanese martial tradition as *kata*. While some Westerners have questioned the necessity for kata training, it continues to form a part of most orthodox martial systems. And the social scientist wonders "why?" This paper examines *kaho* (the use of kata as an instructional tool) from two perspectives: kata training as a cultural activity that has been shaped by the structural characteristics of Japanese culture, and kata training as a highly developed and effective educational mechanism for imparting technical skill in the martial arts.

Practitioners of Motobo-ryu Udun-di, an Okinawan style
as taught by Uehara Seikichi, work together on one
of the nine empty-hand kata in the system.
Photograph courtesy of R. Florence.

Kata

Kata forms the backbone of the Japanese traditional martial arts instructional approach (Friday, 1995; 1997). Popularly understood as "forms," kata are a series of movements combined into a performance set. Most traditional Japanese martial arts organizations and systems have a corpus of individual kata that trainees learn at various points in their study. Mastery of individual kata is often linked to promotion. Thus, kata are most immediately thought of as ways to develop student skill.

Kata are more than just performance routines designed to polish technique or showcase ability, however. They are also thought to embody lessons learned by past masters. When we consider that in feudal Japan a warrior's skill was often proven on the battlefield with lethal finality, the role of kata as non-lethal re-enactments of battlefield experience becomes much more understandable. So, too, can we appreciate the reason proponents of the traditional combat-oriented systems (often identified as *bujutsu*, "martial methods") held kata training in such high regard.

The teaching of combat skill, however, does not necessarily mandate such a highly structured, ritualistic approach. Western wrestlers and boxers, for instance, are not schooled through such elaborate patterns. Westerners practicing more modern martial arts systems have abandoned or de-emphasized kata in favor of what they consider more "realistic" and "practical" exercises. For these people, kata practice is a cultural relic, easily jettisoned. It is a contemporary urge for "relevance" that is quite familiar to educators. Yet kata practice persists in many Japanese martial systems practiced today. This persistence argues for a type of functionality that needs to be examined.

Haruna Matsuo,
a Muso Jikiden Eishin-ryu
instructor, performing a
sword opening and
closing technique.
*Photographs courtesy
of Kim Taylor.*

Cultural Factors

One source of kaho's continued endurance in the martial arts world may spring from the formative cultural environment of the martial arts. The organization of any human activity reflects its cultural context, and the Japanese martial traditions are no exception. Although the mechanics of fighting are considerably conditioned by human physiology and kinesiology, as well as by the weapons technology being applied, stylistic approaches and organizational patterns are culturally conditioned.

Kata are authoritative things. They are passed on from high-ranking instructors to novices. The criteria used to judge the performance of these sets is one that emphasizes a fidelity to form and movement within the dictates the instructor has established. The student's ability to imitate his teacher in kata performance is considered a key to advancement in rank and status. Kaho's stress of hierarchy, authority, organizational belonging, and conformity all resonate strongly with Japanese cultural patterns.

Indeed, in sociological terms, we can understand Japanese martial arts as corporate entities with a strongly hierarchical organization and an explicit ideological charter. These structural factors condition the process of training to a great degree and so bear some further discussion.

In the first place, Japanese martial arts seem to share a predilection for formal organization that can be contrasted to the approach in other Asian countries. From the Tokugawa Period (1603–1868) onward, we note a marked tendency for martial arts training to be organized in corporate entities (Hurst, 1998). Schools came to have both a physical location, the *dojo* (literally "way place," the training hall) as well as a formal identity. Traditional bujutsu systems were often referred to as *ryu* (literally "streams," which gives some sense of the idea of corporate perpetuation). Usage in more modern martial arts systems known as budo is a bit more varied: some systems maintain the ryu label, others use the more modern designation of *kan* (hall) such as in Kodokan judo or Shotokan karatedo, or *kai* (association) as in Kyokushinkai karatedo.

Whatever their labels, these organizations are hierarchical entities, in which issues of rank (related to skill and seniority) condition behavior. At the pinnacle of the organization is the teacher (*sensei*), who is contrasted with his disciples (*montei*). In addition to this gross distinction, there are finer gradations present as well. Students are enmeshed in a dualistic series of relationships between superiors and subordinates that are modeled on the teacher/student split and that echo general structural principles in Japanese society (Nakane, 1970). Thus, a series of relativistic links between seniors (*sempai*) and juniors (*kyohai*) also shapes behavior in the dojo (Donohue, 1991).

The stratified nature of martial arts organizations is reinforced through their well-known ranking systems. Awareness of rank in these organizations is often buttressed by elaborate symbolic means such as methods of address and ritual bowing. In some systems, elements of training uniforms or their color are used to denote status. The most well-known item of clothing associated with rank is the colored-belt system adopted in many modern budo forms. In this system, trainees are classified according to *kyu* (class) and *dan* (grade). While permutations in hue and numbering are almost as varied as schools themselves, beginners in kyu levels usually wear white belts and, as they progress in rank, are awarded a series of different colored belts, culminating in the black belt, a sign that the trainee has reached dan level.

As they are organized today, budo organizations share a commonality with a widespread organizational type in Japan, the *iemoto* ("household origin," the main house in the traditional arts; Hsu, 1975). Although the Japanese do not formally identify most martial arts organizations as iemoto proper, the arts possess the highly structured hierarchical organization based on personal links between masters and disciples that are central characteristics of iemoto organizations.

As formal organizations, martial arts systems also have an explicit ideological charter—a "mission statement" in the corporate jargon of our times. These charters certainly relate to the philosophical orientation of many Japanese martial arts forms. Broadly speaking, many martial arts, and particularly modern budo systems, are inspired by a mix of Shinto, Confucian, and Buddhist ideas that link training with a type of personal/spiritual development. Much has been made, of course, of the alleged link between Zen and the martial arts (Suzuki, 1960; King, 1993; Leggett, 1978). While it is certainly possible that this connection was important for selected martial artists, it is neither universal nor historically accurate.

In fact, while not for a moment calling into question the sincerity of modern martial artists, an objective assessment of martial arts charters reveal them to be vaguely formulated statements that present these arts as ways to advance the technical practice of the art in question, to celebrate human potential, and to advance causes as diffuse and universally unobjectionable as good sportsmanship and world peace. Charters of this type are useful in that they provide an overarching philosophical rationale (however diffuse) for what would otherwise be merely highly stylized calisthenics. In addition, these charters can be understood as the direct consequence of two things: the need to "rehabilitate" the martial arts after the Second World War and a related attempt to homogenize elements of indigenous Japanese ideology so as to be more easily accepted as these arts spread to the West. It is interesting that this diffuse mysticism has had an unexpected appeal for Westerners seeking alternatives to traditional Western belief systems.

Kendo players
utilize kata practice
to maintain realistic
techniques in
a safe way.
*Courtesy of
J. Donohue.*

Traditional Asian approaches to learning may also have reinforced an emphasis on kaho. Friday (1995) suggests that the Confucian infatuation with ritual formalism is at least partly the cause. We might also note that the ideographic Chinese writing system demanded a mastery of literally thousands of characters, and a type of fundamental precision was needed to engage in any literary activity. Given the dominant place of Confucianism in Tokugawa Japan, it is not surprising that the rigor of this approach to instruction informed other endeavors as well.

The modern martial arts, the fundamental characteristics of which were shaped by Tokugawa paradigms, are no exception. All trainees, at whatever level, are expected to continue to practice the building blocks of their particular art for a lifetime. These basic elements form the vocabulary of the martial conversation and, as such, need to be continuously polished. These building blocks tend to be embedded in kata. Many a newly minted karate black belt is surprised, on being awarded dan rank, to being re-introduced to the same kata begun as a white belt. Kaho's stress on repetition, rote learning, and stylistic conformity fit very well within the Confucian tradition.

Rick Polland
practicing a Shindo
Muso-ryu form for
the short staff.
*Courtesy of
R. Polland.*

Dr. Thomas Cauley, Director of the International
Division of Sakugawa Koshiki Shorinji-Ryu
Karate-do, practicing a long staff kata.
A few of his students practicing in unison.
Courtesy of W. Van Horne.

General cultural emphasis on age and seniority also shape kaho. Students tend to learn differing kata in a sequence that is tied to advancement in rank. Their models are "senior" students. And the higher the rank, the more complex the kata and the longer the period of time needed to master it. In the martial arts, there is an explicit belief that the amazing prowess of the master is one that has been forged slowly, over time. It is not a mysterious event. Although it is a supra-rational process, it is the anticipated outcome of practice, refinement, and ruthless self-criticism. The traditional martial arts of Japan reject the "quick and easy" formulations of mass-marketing and run counter to the ostensibly progressive admonitions of Bruce Lee to "absorb what is useful" (1975). The techniques and kata of the art are accepted by trainees as embodying critical martial lessons. The fact that many of these lessons take years to fully grasp does nothing to devalue them. But it once again tends to reinforce a predilection for hierarchy, and kaho fits easily with such an expectation.

Kaho as Technical System

Certainly the traditional reliance on kaho as a centerpiece of training is not a simple cultural relic. The martial arts are as much focused on product—skills development—as they are on process—the constellation of cultural trappings that surround the arts. As "practical arts," we would expect that the retention of kaho reflects a functional appreciation of the method as a pedagogical tool.

A) Pedagogy

We may posit that kaho must be an extremely flexible instructional tool to survive in the modern dojo. In the first place, we must remind ourselves that martial arts study is voluntary. While school children in Japan are still required to take judo or kendo in school, further training is a result of individual initiative. And in the West, martial arts training halls fall squarely within the category of "voluntary organizations." Participation presupposes a willingness to study, often because of some perceived benefit. But the motivations for training are as varied as the trainees themselves, and so may be the levels of ability. This mandates a flexible technique for teaching that may be one element in ensuring the continuing importance of kaho.

Some students approach the martial arts as exotic forms of exercise. Those of us who have trained in these arts for any length of time, after inventorying the bruises, broken bones, etc. involved may wonder whether there are other activities that create less wear and tear, but it remains that many consider martial arts training a calisthenic activity.

In the West, the allure of fighting skills development often forms a part in martial arts marketing. We might note in passing that this idea is not seriously entertained in Japan. But for Westerners, the hint of Asian mystery and the promise of arcane mastery embodied in every cheap B-grade martial arts movie keeps this questionable self-defense motivation alive. Other students are attracted by the vague yet comfortably exotic ideological trappings of some martial arts systems. They seek a sort of experiential transcendence in their training.

All of which suggests that the student body of a typical martial arts dojo is extremely heterogeneous in terms of personal motivation and athletic ability. This complicates issues relating to "practical" activities such as sparring, where questions of size, strength, endurance, willingness to experience pain, etc. are highly variable. The need for a mechanism for imparting the fundamentals of a particular system, while not introducing unwanted or undue stress on trainees, may well account for an emphasis on kata in training. We note that the more competitive modern forms of the martial arts—that is, those systems that rigidly segregate trainees into classes of higher and lower competencies and are composed of aggressive personalities—are ones that have drifted away from a heavy reliance on kaho as an instructional method.

In addition, we must also remember that the pace of this process of mastery is determined by the individual pupil's aptitude. Martial arts training displays no temporal structure to the training cycle, and entering cohorts are quickly eroded by the notoriously high drop-out rates within dojos. In addition, training may be considered a "spiral" rather than lineal process: trainees continue to refine even the most elemental skills throughout their training careers. Differing physical capacities, levels of emotional maturity, and psychological factors create varying dynamics for each student. Any experienced martial arts instructor knows that there are fairly consistent patterns in aggregate learning, but that each student brings a unique set of strengths and weaknesses to the process. The cyclical nature of training using kata thus permits general progression to take place while at the same time permitting individual focus on specific deficiencies.

Kata practice is also an activity that can be engaged in alone or by groups of students of various age levels or competencies—a key point stressed by modernizers such as Funakoshi Gichin (1868–1957). As such, it is a technique ideally suited to maximizing teachability among heterogeneous populations, an important consideration when we consider the activity's voluntary nature and its existence within a market context.

B) Practicality

There are also basic issues relating to "crowd control" and safety that recommend kaho. It was considered essential in the *kobujutsu*, the old systems of Japan, which are heavily weapons oriented. In addition to the cultural influences cited earlier, the extreme lethality of edged weapons introduces complications in the teaching method: training must be as realistic as possible, but not induce casualties among the trainees. The mechanics of controlling a class of novices wielding razor sharp or heavy wooden weapons suggests that kaho permitted a replication of successful combat techniques in a choreographed manner.

A room full of students using a slashing weapon like the Japanese sword (*katana*), for instance, provides some real and very serious immediate practical considerations. The wind up and finish embodied in techniques using a three-foot sword create a zone of danger around each swordsman. Trainees need to learn critical issues regarding distance and safe management of the weapon. They need to learn to wield their weapons well and to avoid those of their fellow students. This is not a trivial concern. Note that the sorts of weapons typically used in the martial arts are characteristic of individual, heroic combat styles. The greater the density of fighters in one spot, the higher the likelihood of a literal type of collateral damage. Armies that utilize mass formations tend to emphasize thrusting attacks, since they focus danger to the front and toward the enemy and minimize the possibility of self-inflicted wounds. The techniques developed for the Roman legionnaire's gladius, the Zulu impi's assegai, and the Greek hoplite's spears and swords all support this observation. Japan's weapons systems, forged in a different age, provide unique problems for group practice.

Viewed from this perspective, we can understand kaho's practical aspect as something driven by the need to create a pattern of behavior that protects students from themselves and each other, as well as one that provides an environment in which instructions for complex skills can be communicated, despite the emotional overlay of excitement, fear, and effort.

As mentioned before, kata are also models of success. They are thought to embody lessons learned by past masters. Like all cultural learning, they serve as a type of compacted, highly condensed information stream that holds multiple lessons for practitioners. Thus, kata can be used to teach the rudiments of a system, to refine growing skill, and also to reveal more subtle applications (*bunkai*) to advanced practitioners.

Katas have both cultural and technical influences, and are practices for form and function. Above, Mr. Giles Hopkins illustrates a Goju-Ryu solo form.

Katas have both cultural and technical
influences, and are practices for form
and function. Mr. Giles Hopkins illustrates
a Goju-Ryu solo form (above), and its
application from the Saifa kata (below).
Courtesy of G. Hopkins.

C) Ideas and Emotions

In more modern martial arts forms, the emphasis on kata is also driven by ideological factors that seek to create a mind-set that is not solely focused on com-

students—their attitude as much as their aptitude—and kata practice can serve as an excellent vehicle to do so.

There is also an additional ritual and aesthetic quality to kata performance. The stereotyped movements replicated through kata performance may be understood to be doing a number of things: they serve as a public statement of adherence to a particular martial arts style, they are a visible indicator of an individual's acquisition of skill, they provide the opportunity to experience a "flow" experience directly linked to the mystical-religious aspects of the martial arts that attract so many Westerners, and, to the extent that performance is skillful, it draws both observers and performers into an aesthetic community that identifies and reaffirms basic underlying systemic principles.

Conclusion

Westerners tend to view kaho as a cultural relic. Its persistence as a teaching tool in the Japanese martial tradition, however, may suggest that there is a functionality present in the method that is often overlooked. As with most sociological phenomena, there is a complex network of influences at play here.

The tradition of kaho is shaped by two major categories of influences: the cultural and the technical. Cultural patterns inherent in East Asian society during the formative period of martial arts development certainly account for some aspects of these systems: clothing, terminology, etiquette, and even kata practice. This is not, however, the only element at play here.

The fighting systems' overwhelmingly "practical" nature suggests that more mundane factors may be at play. We have identified pedagogical issues that support a continued utilization of kaho, practical considerations that are created by the nature of the human/weapon interface, and more psychological aspects that serve to answer more complex emotional needs of practitioners. It is hoped that the exercise, like the practice of kata itself, assists in revealing the sophisticated and complex nature of these martial systems.

Bibliography

Budden, P. (2000). *Looking at a far mountain: A study of kendo kata*. Rutland, VT: Tuttle Publishing.

Craig, D. (1999). *The heart of kendo*. Boston: Shambhala.

Csikszentmihalyi, M. (1990). *Flow: The psychology of optimal experience*. New York: Harper and Row.

Csikszentmihalyi, M. (1975). *Beyond boredom and anxiety: The experience of play and work in games*. San Francisco, CA: Josey-Bass.

Donohue, J. (1991). The dimensions of discipleship: Organizational paradigm, mystical transmission, and vested interest in the Japanese martial tradition. *Ethnos*, 55, 1–2.

Friday, K., with Humitake, S. (1997). *Legacies of the sword: The Kashima Shin-ryu and samurai martial culture*. Honolulu: University of Hawaii Press.

Friday, K. (1995). Kabala in motion: Kata and pattern practice in traditional bugei. *Journal of Asian Martial Arts*, 4(4), 27–39.

Hanson, V. (1989). *The western way of war: Infantry battle in classical Greece*. Berkeley, CA: University of California Press.

Hsu, F. (1975). *Iemoto: The heart of Japan*. Cambridge: Belknap Press.

Hurst, G. (1998). *Armed martial arts of Japan: Swordsmanship and archery*. New Haven, CT: Yale University Press.

Inoue Y. (2002a). A philosophical look at kata. *Kendo World*, 1(2), 34–38.

Inoue Y. (2002b). The philosophy of kata: Part 2. *Kendo World*, 1(3), 59–69.

Kawaishi, M. (1982). *The complete 7 katas of judo*. Woodstock, NY: Overlook-Press.

Kano, J. (1986). *Kodokan judo*. Tokyo: Kodansha International.

King, W. (1993). *Zen and the way of the sword: Arming the samurai psyche*. Oxford: Oxford University Press.

Lee, B. (1975). *The tao of Jeet Kun Do*. Burbank, CA: Ohara Publishing.

Leggett, T. (1978). *Zen and the ways*. Rutland, VT: Charles E. Tuttle Co.

Morris, D. (1965). *The washing of the spears*. New York: Simon and Schuster.

Nakane, C. (1970). *Japanese society*. Berkeley, CA: University of California Press.

Onuma, H., with De Prospero, D., & De Prospero, J. (1993). *Kyudo: The essence and practice of Japanese archery*. Tokyo: Kodansha International.

Otaki, T., & Draeger, D. (1983). *Judo formal techniques: A complete guide to Kodokan Randori no Kata*. Rutland, VT: Charles E. Tuttle Co.

Suzuki, D. (1959). *Zen and Japanese culture*. Princeton, NJ: Princeton University Press.

Warner, G., & Draeger, D. (1982). *Japanese swordsmanship: Theory and practice*. Tokyo: Weatherhill.

Elements of Advanced
Karate Techniques

by Marvin Labbate

Photographs courtesy of M. Labbate.

Every karate student is endowed with a level of strength, speed, flexibility, and endurance that with time and practice naturally develops. Unfortunately, these superficial qualities often mark the primary difference between the beginner and the advanced black belt. This chapter focuses on elements of a deeper subject: the lifelong development of technique. To illustrate the process of development, the chapter probes deeply into the first four steps of Sanchin, the most fundamental kata of Okinawan Goju-ryu.

The version of Sanchin discussed here was developed by the style's founder, Miyagi Chojun, and serves primarily as a catalog of basic principles. It evolved by adding hard (*go*) closed-handed, strength building movements to soft (*ju*), open-handed techniques imported from China. Miyagi taught Sanchin as the first kata and considered it so important that he required students to train exclusively in it for many years. When performed correctly, Sanchin harmonizes both the soft and hard components of structure, movement, and breathing. The goal of this paper is to systematically reveal these principles by explaining the kata at successively deeper levels of understanding. At the beginner level, the soft principles of Sanchin are introduced and developed. At the intermediate level, hard principles are added. Finally, the advanced student develops the combination of soft and hard to achieve the desired training outcome and improve overall technique. The ideas are so fundamental that they are applicable to any karate style and every student can benefit from the study of Sanchin.

Principles of Structure and Movement

The beginning student focuses attention on the principles of structure and movement in Sanchin. This involves memorization of the basic pattern, correct positioning and movement of the body, and harmonizing breathing with motion. The kata should be performed repeatedly each day in front of a mirror, and always with the gi top removed to allow careful inspection of the body's position and form. The beginner uses slow, graceful, tension-free movements and follows each move by checking the body position and adjusting the stance to the correct form.

Principle #1
Practice slowly and carefully, checking and correcting stance with each movement.

The mind should be focused using the same procedure with each stance: it begins by placing attention at the feet and works steadily up the body until reaching the *tanden*, a spot located just below the navel that forms the center of energy flow in the body. Focus is then moved to the crown point at the top of the head and continues down the body ending again at the tanden. This procedure ensures that each muscle group is considered methodically as part of a consistent procedure of improvement.

Principle #2
Focus the mind on each muscle group in a fixed pattern.

Sanchin uses a simple pattern that combines several basic blocks and punches. An overview of the complete kata can be found in Higaonna Morio's highly recommended book (1987). The sequence below shows the movements taken from the ready-stance (*heiko dachi*, 1A). The first transition is to a right sanchin stance (*migi sanchin dachi*) and is followed by a double-handed side block (*morote chudan yoko uke*, 1B). Following the block, the left hand is chambered (1C), a left two-knuckle punch (*hidari seiken zuki*, 1D) is executed, then a left side block (1E). These movements are followed by a step into a left sanchin stance, the right hand is chambered, and a right two-knuckle punch with corresponding side block is executed.

The sequence continues, as shown below starting with 1F, with a step into a right sanchin stance executing a corresponding left chamber (1F) and punch (1G). The left hand is then rechambered (1H) and brought across the body while the student looks at an adversary on the left (1I). The right foot then transitions in a crosslegged stance (1J), a 180-degree turn is executed (1K), and the student ends in a left sanchin stance with the right hand chambered. This sequence sets the student up to repeat the basic pattern of three steps and punches in the opposite direction.

Opening Steps of
Sanchin Kata

Structure

Applying principle #2, let us now re-examine the central aspects of the opening sequence from the viewpoint of structure. Consider the ready stance shown previously in 1A and begin at the feet: The feet form our link to the universe; our goal is to firmly root the body to the floor and lower the body's center of gravity to provide stability. To achieve this, the position of the feet is critical. Photo 2A shows the correct positioning with the outer edges of the feet parallel, shoulders' width apart.

Ready Stance Feet Positioning

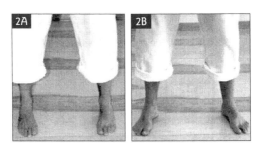

A common error is to position the feet in the more natural stance (2B). Unfortunately, a stable stance cannot be obtained from this position. The same concept applies to the sanchin stance shown throughout the opening sequence. As in the ready stance, careful positioning of the feet is essential to stability. Photo 2C shows the correct positioning for a right sanchin stance. The toe of the left foot and heel of the right foot are aligned, shoulders' width apart. The left foot is aligned with the outer edge forward and the right foot is turned slightly inward. A common error is to position the feet as shown in 2D; again, a stable stance cannot be obtained in this position.

Sanchin Stance Feet Positioning

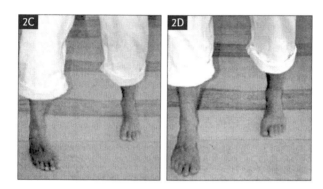

Principle #3

Correctly position the feet so as to grip the floor.

Working up the body, the hips should be carefully aligned facing forward with the back held straight above the base of the spine. Moving to the top of the body, the crown of the head is pushed upward as if to suck energy from the universe while straightening the neck and spine. The eyes look forward and slightly upward, as if looking to the future. When performing in front of a mirror, the gaze should be turned over the right shoulder of the reflection so as to allow the entire body to be perceived at once using peripheral vision. The tongue is placed on the hard palate allowing the free flow of air to and from the body. The chin is tucked slightly inward to improve breathing and prevent strangle holds. The shoulders are always aligned forward and held down.

Notice the position of the arms and shoulders in the double side block in photo 1B. The elbow is placed a fist's distance from the body and the arm forms a 90 degree angle at the elbow. The arms form a "V" shape in front of the body with the shoulders firmly down.

Principle #4

Use peripheral vision to take in the entire scene.

Principle #5

Correctly position the arms to ensure an effective blocking technique that will deflect rather than forcibly stop a blow.

Movement

There are four primary transitions in the opening sequence:

1) stance-to-stance
2) chamber-to-punch
3) punch-to-block
4) stance-to-turn.

The goal of the beginning student is to remain fluid, stable and upright at all times with the shoulders held down and the hips and shoulders aligned forward. The body does not sway from side to side, nor bob up and down while in motion. To achieve this fluidity the body is held loose with the knees slightly bent.

Principle #6

Move gracefully with circular motions paying special attention to keep the body from bobbing up and down or swaying from side to side.

The stance-to-stance transition occurs between the ready stance and sanchin stance (1A and 1B), or between consecutive sanchin stances. This transition is achieved by moving the body's weight to the forward foot while bending the forward knee slightly to keep the shoulders at the same level. The rear foot is then brought forward in a circular motion that extends to the centerline between the feet. The foot that moves maintains contact with the floor on its outer edge throughout the motion. At the end of the transition the feet are checked to ensure that they are positioned correctly. If an error is found, the foot that moved is the one that made the mistake; corrections are therefore always applied to the foot that moved.

The chamber-to-punch transition shown in photos 1C and 1D is broken down into five segments (in 3A through 3E). The transition begins from the chambered position in which the elbow points down and the hand is clenched with the thumb tucked to prevent an inadvertent break (3A). The punch first extends to an uppercut position (3B), then transitions to a vertical punch when the elbow is approximately a fist distance from the body (3C). When the punch is fully extended, it rests in a natural position slightly inward from the vertical position. This position is best determined though a simple arm swinging exercise: swing the arms loosely at the side of the body extending up to shoulder height; after swinging freely four or five times, halt the swing at shoulder height and the hands will naturally hold the correct striking position. The chamber-to-punch transition ends with a cutting motion of the hand when the arm is fully extended. This final movement occurs after the blow is struck and causes the knuckles to grind into an opponent with a twisting motion. The transition ends with the arm locked into its final position (3E).

Chamber-to-Punch Transition

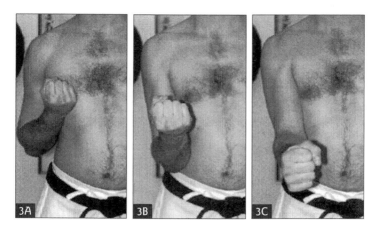

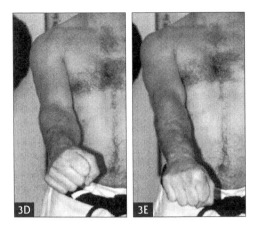

The punch extends forward from the shoulder, like a battering ram, and does not cross the body. In this manner, the punch is delivered with the full weight of the body behind it. When striking an opponent, the practitioner aligns the body to strengthen the punch rather than weaken it to compensate for poor positioning. Throughout this sequence, the shoulders remain firmly down, the upper arm pinches the pectoral muscles, and the elbow transitions by scraping the rib cage. Two common errors are to raise the shoulders and to allow the elbow to drift outward from the body. Both weaken the technique. It is most important to practice the punch very slowly until it becomes second nature.

The punch-to-block transition follows a circular path much like opening a door: the hand rotates upward while the elbow moves in slightly, causing the upper arm to push against the pectoral muscles. Throughout the transition, the shoulders remain down and the final body position should again be with the forearms in a V-shape with the elbows a fist's distance from the body.

The final transition, stance-to-turn, is shown in photos 1J and 1K and requires that the body remain upright at all times. As the right leg crosses the left, the knees should touch. The turn is performed on the balls of the feet in a manner that ends in sanchin stance. As the body twists out of the turn, the left arm first forms a guard and then moves into the standard side block position, while the right arm is simultaneously chambered in readiness for a punch.

Principle #7

All punches develop from a common
transition in which the arm extends forward
from the shoulder like a battering ram.

Principle #8

During all movements, the shoulders are
held down, the upper arm pinches the pectoral
muscles, and the elbows scrape the rib cage.

Breathing

The beginning student uses natural abdominal breathing (*zhengfu huxi* in Mandarin) taken from internal energy work (*neidan qigong* in Mandarin, *kiko* in Japanese). Unlike normal breathing that involves movement of the chest, natural breathing uses a slow, deep, abdominal breath centered on the tanden (*dantian* in Mandarin). The abdomen is consciously forced to expand as air is inhaled through the nose. The abdomen is allowed to contract as air is exhaled through the mouth. The breath is never held, but instead circulates in a continuous, smooth and natural motion. This form of breathing is used to heal the body and develop physical strength. It has the effect of exercising and developing the abdominal muscles; massaging the internal organs, especially the kidneys; and increasing circulation. This process calms the mind, strengthens the will, and leads to a general improvement in health that allows the student to progress to develop other aspects of technique.

A particularly crucial concept in Sanchin kata is to synchronize breathing with movement. This synchronization manages oxygen to ensure that techniques are always delivered with the full force of mind and body. Consider the initial few movements of the kata from the ready stance shown in the "1" sequence of photos. The first motion, to the double side block, is accompanied by a long breath. The inhalation occurs while the hands rise; the student exhales as the arms fall into position in the double side block. This sets up the breathing pattern for subsequent moves that are generally prepared with inhalation and delivered with exhalation. The subsequent punch is delivered with a long deep breath. While chambering the left hand for the punch, as shown in photo 1C, inhalation begins at the point where movement to the chamber is initiated and stops at the precise moment that the hand is in its final resting position in the chamber. Exhalation begins when the punch is initiated; the breath is fully expelled precisely at the point where the punch ends as shown in photo 1D. The subsequent side block, photo 1E, involves a short breath. As the arm rotates upward, inhalation occurs; breath is exhaled as the arm falls into position in the standard double block.

One further example of this synchronization occurs in the final stance-to-turn transition shown in photos 1H through 1K. The breath is inhaled while the left hand is chambered (1H), then exhaled while it traverses the body (1-I) and inhaled for the full duration of the turn (1J and 1K). This sequence ensures that oxygen is available for a subsequent punch with the chambered right hand.

Principle #9

Synchronize natural breathing with motion: inhale while preparing and exhale while delivering each blow.

Intermediate Go Principles

After learning the basic pattern combining structure with movement and breathing, the intermediate student progresses to strength training. In gongfu parlance this has been termed "iron-shirt training," as it gradually develops a hard surface of solid muscle that provides protection against even the strongest blows. The essence of the idea is to gradually reinforce the basic structures introduced earlier by adding successive levels of muscular tension, thereby building strength and endurance. A central component of this training is to lock down each muscle group into a strong reinforced position with each movement.

At the intermediate level, Sanchin is performed slowly and carefully with all muscle groups in tension and constant attention to form. A common error is for the student to exaggerate the required tension with severe and uncontrollable exertion. Over-exertion can lead to high blood pressure and cause a heart attack or stroke. Further, a muscle under severe exertion tires the student and results in jerky motions. In contrast, a tight solid muscle can provide protection and yet be moved with fluidity. Muscular tension is built gradually over a period of years, through repetition.

Structure

Returning to the right sanchin stance (1B), the mind is focused to induce tension by considering each muscle group in turn as focus moves up the body. With the feet in the position shown in photo 2A, the toes grip the floor while the heels turn inward rooting the stance in the floor and gripping it tightly. Focus then moves to the calves and backs of the legs, which should be tightened by a twisting motion at the heels. Then focus turns to the thighs, with the knees bent slightly; the anus is tucked inward; and the tanden is moved upward slightly. This causes the thighs to tighten in an outward twisting motion that protects the groin and places the entire lower body in tension. A common error is for the student to lean backward when performing this technique. The back must be kept straight with the hips aligned forward for stability. A graphic illustration of poor technique can be obtained by attempting this procedure with the feet in the position shown in photo

2B: the feet are unable to gain a firm grip in this position and, as a result, little tightening of the body is possible.

Moving now to the top of the body: the crown of the head is pushed upward, the neck becomes tense, and the shoulders, which should be down, also become tense. In the double block position, the top of the arm pinches the pectoral muscles causing the entire muscle group at the shoulder to be locked down into position as shown in photo "4". Next, the hands are clenched firmly, the elbow is moved inward slightly and the small finger on each hand is rotated toward the body. These motions place tension on every muscle group in both the upper and lower arm. Finally, moving further down the body, the muscles in the abdomen at the tanden are tightened.

Upper Arm Pinching the Pectoral Muscles

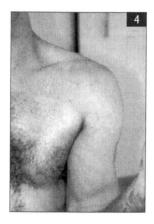

Supplemental Weight Training

To perfect locking of the muscles in the upper body, training is augmented with chishi weights, such as those shown in photos 5A through 5E. If these weights are not available, students can obtain a heavy sledgehammer from a local hardware store and simply cut down the handle to obtain a training device with the same characteristics. Chishi training is initiated by simply placing the device on the floor in front of the student (5A). The student then wraps a hand around the handle and lifts the weight vertically by bending the knees and keeping the arm straight (5B). This first movement places the shoulder muscle group in the correct locked position: it should feel as if the entire shoulder from the neck, across the pectoral muscles, and into the upper arm is one complete and integrated whole. Next, the chishi is brought upward to position (5C). This position corresponds to a vertical punch. The student should again feel the upper arm pinching against the pectoral muscles and again the entire shoulder group should lock down into an integrated whole. From the vertical punch, the chishi is then brought to the side block position (5D). This position again locks the shoulder group, but also causes the elbow to be rotated across the body and the small finger of the hand to be rotated inward causing the entire set of arm muscles to become tense and unified. To end the exercise, the chishi is brought backward, then over the shoulder and back to the vertical punch position (5E). During this motion, the student attempts to maintain the shoulder group in a locked position. This motion is repeated on each side and eventually with two weights simultaneously. A variety of other similar exercises can be used to enhance this form of training.

Chishi Training

Chishi training can be based on repetitions to strengthen the shoulder muscle group in every position used and improve endurance. Alternatively, training can be conducted slowly with each position held so as to develop endurance, flexibility and form. Slow training is used to feel the muscles working: The student holds each position, closes the eyes, and focuses the mind on allowing the weight to take the muscle group to a natural position. The weight works to assemble the muscle group in the correct position and allows the student to develop an instinctive feel for the correct position. When performing the kata, this instinctive feeling will guide the positioning of the body and lead to improved technique without conscious thought.

Progress in chishi training is immediately noticeable from the manner in which the student picks up the chishi as shown in photos 5A and 5B. Early on, the student picks up the chishi with the arm muscles and tires the arm quickly. Soon this movement progresses to where the weight is lifted with the entire shoulder group locked into position. Eventually the student lifts the weight with the entire body: the body is rooted in the floor providing a stable position, the center of weight is lowered, the anus is tucked, and all of the other Sanchin principles are applied.

Principle #10

Lock each muscle group into a single integrated
whole that is maintained throughout the kata.

Movement

The muscle locking techniques developed using chishi weights are integrated directly into the performance of Sanchin kata. Throughout each movement, the student pays careful attention to the body's position to ensure that all muscle groups are locking into the appropriate positions. Every movement of the arms, be it punch, block or chamber, should occur with the shoulders down and the entire upper body configured as a single muscle mass.

The student focuses attention on the shoulder group during each punch. As the punch extends, the elbow scrapes the rib cage. The pectoral muscles and upper arm grip tightly together causing a pinching of the muscles just below the armpit. The punch extends like a battering ram with every arm muscle locked into position supporting the arm. The entire weight of the body strikes the punch, not simply the knuckles. To illustrate this point, the student can try extending a punch with the focus of attention at the knuckles. The effect is to loosen the entire arm and shoulder muscle group; this results in a punch that has little force and cohesiveness.

With the body under tension, any movement of the feet inevitably causes a momentary loss of the body's rooting in the floor. As a result, the foot movements between techniques are deliberately quicker and somewhat jerkier than the slow and deliberate movements of the arms. The intent is to minimize the loss of tension during transitions.

Breathing

At the intermediate level, the student begins to learn an alternative abdominal breathing technique called "martial breathing" (*fanfu huxi* in Mandarin). Like natural breathing, this form strengthens and develops the abdominal muscles and provides substantially more oxygen to the body than everyday breathing. Two primary forms of this breathing technique are employed in Sanchin kata. The first is a long deep breath in which air is drawn in slowly and deeply through the nose. The breath is visualized as following a long path around the top of the head, down the neck and back, under the groin, and finally curls itself up at the tanden in the lower abdomen. This long and deep abdominal breath inward is accompanied by the abdomen contracting. When exhaling, air is pushed out as the abdomen expands. The air moves slowly and smoothly, rising up the front of the body to the neck, and is finally expelled through the mouth.

The second form of breathing is a short breath in which air is transferred directly to the tanden while the abdomen contracts. The breath is expended quickly and directly while the abdomen expands. Just as in natural breathing, all breathing is synchronized with the motion of the body when performing the kata. Once again, breath is inhaled when preparing a technique and exhaled when delivering it.

The intermediate student develops the martial breathing pattern to store a reserve of oxygen and to lower the body's center of mass. The chest never moves during this form of breathing since all breath is concentrated in the tanden.

During exhalation, as breath is pushed out of the abdomen, the breath is cut short at about 75 percent with a "ha" sound that originates in the abdomen. This sound is synchronized with a conscious tightening of the abdominal muscles. These muscles tighten first outward and then downward as the student's attention is on the abdomen, lowering the body's center of weight. At the same time, the associated technique is locked into position as described in previous sections. For example, at the precise moment that a punch strikes, the shoulder group should become locked, breath is 75 percent expelled, and the muscles in the abdomen are pushed down, the lower body is tightened, and the body becomes rooted into the floor. The technique thus drives into an opponent's body like a battering ram from a highly stable position with the entire body rigid just at the instant of impact.

Principle #11

Combine martial breathing
and locking to obtain solid
and highly stable striking
and defensive forms.

During an attack, the body is most vulnerable between breaths since generally there is little oxygen to power movement. This form of martial breathing ensures that the body always carries a reserve of breath with which to respond. Moreover, no visual clue can be taken from the motion of the chest as to the breathing pattern, making it difficult for an opponent to time an attack between breaths. Finally, tightening of the abdominal muscles allows the body to accept a blow to the body with a reserve of oxygen to power a counterattack.

The effect of conscious movement of weight into the tanden can be demonstrated with a simple test. A second person attempts to lift the student, first without weight focused into the tanden and subsequently with the appropriate focus. In the former case, it is relatively easy to lift the student from the ground; in the latter it is nearly impossible. The conscious lowering of the center of weight, coupled with the rooting of the body in the ground by applying tension in the lower body, leads to unparalleled stability. It is generally not possible to dislodge the practitioner from the sanchin stance even with violent thrusts.

Advanced Goju-Ryu Techniques

The advanced practitioner builds upon the basic concepts described previously by combining both the hard and soft principles to stress a particular component of technique during a single training session. It is important to develop a number of refinements to the basic concepts.

Building and Controlling Energy

Over the centuries, the Chinese have developed a theory of how the human body interacts with the universe and how energy (*qi*; *ki* in Japanese) is developed, stored, and expended in the human body. The theory is based on the opposing and complementary forces in nature (yin and yang) and attempts to develop an understanding of the human body from this viewpoint. Central to this study is a system of vital energy points and meridians that represent paths of energy flow between major points and organs in the body. For example, one of the primary energy points is the tanden, translated as the "field of elixir," reflecting the vital role that oxygen and breathing play in physical well being. The study of energy flow is a recurrent theme in Daoist philosophy and underlies traditional Chinese medicine and healing practices, such as acupuncture. To master and improve the energy flow in the body, physical disciplines have evolved, such as yoga and qigong, that develop the interaction of movement, breathing, and mental concentration. These healing concepts are the foundation upon which the martial arts are built. Many exercises in karate work and develop specific meridians. Therefore, it should not be surprising that advanced karate attempts to focus the flow and transfer of energy into martial techniques.

To illustrate how energy is built and controlled, reconsider the initial sequence of movements in Sanchin. After the initial double block shown in photo 1B, the first punch (1D) is performed under increased tension brought about by mental focus. When the next block follows (1E), tension is again increased. This action effectively locks stored energy into the right side of the body. As the left punch and block are subsequently developed, concentration is again focused on increasing tension in the body, this time locking down both shoulder muscle groups. Both sides of the body are now under heightened tension, storing energy. The final punch and block combination, on the right side of the body, further reenforces and increases this tension. Thus, just prior to the turn, the body should feel like a pressure cooker storing energy.

As the feet are positioned for the turn, a subtle modification is made to the hip position as illustrated in photo 6. Instead of holding them in an aligned position, the hips are twisted in the direction opposite to the turn. This maintains the stored energy in the body and should feel as if the body is being coiled up like a spring. When the turn is finally executed, it occurs at very high speed, as if the spring were suddenly released, causing all the stored energy of previous movements to be thrown sharply into the block that follows the turn. Imagine receiving this block on any part of the anatomy; it would be a blow of devastating impact.

The Coiled Spring

Miyagi Chojun believed that a conflict should be ended with the first block. Clearly, a block is not simply a defensive technique. It can be highly effective in immobilizing an opponent when performed with sufficient energy.

Principle #12

Carefully build and control the expenditure of energy.

Fajing

As a student develops the ability to build and control internal energy, techniques must then be developed to transfer power (*fajing* in Mandarin) into karate techniques. To illustrate this, consider how power can be transferred into the punching technique. In the previous explanations, emphasis was on maintaining the hips aligned forward during the performance of the Sanchin kata. Careful consideration of this position will develop an instinct for the final locked position of each movement. However, the power of a punch comes not from the motion of the arm, but from placing the body weight behind the punch. This motion originates in a subtle movement of the hips that is exaggerated in photos 7A and 7B. This sequence breaks down the motion of the punch and highlights the associated hip movement. Throughout the delivery of a punch, the hips lead the body's movement. Just at the point of contact, the entire body reverberates back into the locked position practiced previously, with the hips aligned. In this position, the shoulder muscles are locked down, the arm is aligned with the body in the battering ram position, the body is firmly rooted into the ground, 75 percent of the body's air has been expelled, and the abdominal muscles are tensed.

Efficient hip motion cannot be achieved without careful practice. Three exercises are useful in developing fajing. The first involves the free motion of the hips: The student stands upright in the ready stance, the arms are held loosely by the sides, and the hips are swung freely from left to right by turning the body. The shoulders are held parallel to the floor and the swing is exaggerated as far to the left and right as possible to ensure the free motion of the body.

Hip Movement During Punching

In the second exercise, the body is rotated in a similar fashion to the first. However, here the movement is driven from the hips with a shaking movement. The shaking of the body is driven from the hip motion rather than being carried by the twisting of the body. The hip motion should be allowed to die down naturally after two or three shakes from left to right. The initial thrust of the hips eventually reverberates back to an aligned position naturally. Good posture must be maintained throughout these exercises.

In the final exercise, the hip is thrust forward, the body shakes, and eventually comes to a final locked position in which the body is tense and rooted in the ground as described previously at the end of the punch. Over a period of time, the hip motion becomes second nature and is gradually integrated into the overall punching technique. As practice proceeds, the hip motion should become less and less pronounced. It eventually blends into a fluid body motion associated with every punch or block. At this time, fajing becomes an internal component of the motion of the tanden rather than an observable external movement.

Principle #13

Strike not with the hand.
but with the entire
body through fajing.

Loading and Reloading

Each technique in the opening sequence has so far been explained somewhat independently. However, the kata can be used to leverage the yin and yang concept of force and counterforce by loading and reloading the body's energy for subsequent movements. This ki control allows every cover and chamber to reload the energy in the body for a subsequent block or strike respectively through a subtle positioning of the body. For example, following a right punch and block the body is locked down into position with the hips aligned. As the left arm is brought to the chamber position, the hips move back slightly, loading the body with energy for the subsequent punch. This principle can also be applied to every block. Generally, each block has an associated cover. Hip movement during the cover has the function of loading energy into the block. The block is executed with fajing, causing the stored energy to be transferred directly into the block and thus increasing the force of the technique.

Principle #14

Load and reload the body's energy to
cascade a sequence of techniques.

Concluding Remarks

Sanchin is not a fighting kata, but rather a catalog of principles that develops general technique. These principles permeate all aspects of karate and are the basis for all other kata. For example, every kata involves a variety of stances that include the ready stance, forward stance, etc. In every stance, we can apply the basic principles from Sanchin: The feet are positioned so as to grip the floor. Circular movements are used in each transition to protect vital parts of the body. The feet remain in contact with the floor at all times, preventing sweeps and throws. Each movement is conducted with fluidity; however, at the split second of delivery, each block or punch takes the form of Sanchin. The feet provide stability by being rooted to the ground. Each punch is delivered as a battering ram with the force of the body behind it, and every muscle group locked to reinforce the blow. Each block is itself a blow that sets up the body for a subsequent technique by loading ki into the body for the counterstrike. Breathing is coordinated with movements to conserve energy in the body and extend endurance. Clearly, Sanchin is the source of all these concepts.

The heightened role of discipline in Asian culture allows students to actively pursue Sanchin concepts without the need for reasoning. In stark contrast, students in the United States are conditioned by their heritage to strive for understanding through questioning. The western mind is unable to focus on the "how" of an activity, unless there is first a clear understanding of the "why" that underlies it. This basic cultural difference is often misunderstood and presents a significant barrier to karate students in the United States. As a result, much of the advanced training that occurs only after the attainment of a black belt in Okinawa is lost on US practitioners. This article has sought to reveal some of the principles and reasons why students should pursue Sanchin training with diligence: it will surely lead to superior technique and will carryover to every aspect of their martial arts training, irrespective of the style chosen to pursue.

Reference

Higaonna, M. (1987). *The traditional karate-do — Okinawan Goju Ryu, vol. 2: Performances of the kata.* Tokyo: Japan Publications.

Developing Advanced Goju-Ryu Techniques: Illustrated in the Rising Block

by Marvin Labbate

All photographs courtesy of M. Labbate

Introduction

The difference in skills between a beginning and an advanced karate student should be marked by more than levels of strength, speed, flexibility and endurance. These qualities can be improved with time and practice. This chapter considers something deeper concerning the lifelong development of technique. The focus here is on the principles of advanced blocking techniques in Okinawan Goju-ryu and their associated applications. This chapter builds upon the core principles of structure, movement, and breathing developed in a previous chapter on Sanchin kata (Labbate, 1999). The standard rising block is used as a vehicle to explain blocking principles, however, the ideas apply to all of the standard blocks.

In common with other blocks used in traditional karate, the rising block has often been criticized as an ineffective fighting technique. Although this criticism is justified at the beginner's level, the advanced practitioner develops a qualitatively different technique. The advanced level block transfers internal energy into the block from the center of the body, uses inner sensitivity to intercept, adhere, and redirect an opponent's energy, and body-shifting to gain a position of advantage. Correct distancing, timing, and hand-eye coordination are developed through partner training. The final block is a combination of hard and soft principles that allows it to serve a broad variety of defensive and offensive applications.

The Beginner's Level

Beginning students are generally taught a mechanical rising block that allows them to develop the gross movement and coordinate their arms (Oyama, 1981). This basic block is shown in Sequence 1. From the ready position (1A), the student transitions to a simple covering position (1B), then forms a cross with the covering arm and the blocking arm (1C), and finishes with a lifting motion in which the blocking arm rotates into its final position, a fist distance from the forehead (1D). The covering position provides a first line of defense while the lifting motion is

supposed to force an opponent's punch upward and away from the face. Unfortunately, this lifting motion is useless against a powerful opponent who will simply punch right through the intended block with a direct strike to the face.

Building on this basic block, intermediate level skills are then taught in which the student begins to develop the ability to deflect while blocking. In this block, rather than crossing the covering arm with the blocking arm, the blocking arm takes a direct 45-degree path from the chamber to its final position. Although slightly more difficult to grasp, this alternative block deflects an opponent's punch rather than opposes its force. The intermediate block is practiced in both stationary and moving two-person blocking (*tanshiki*) drills where the defending student steps backward to block an attacker's blow. These two-person drills provide reflexive training and begin to develop hand–eye coordination, timing, speed, and distancing.

Building further upon the intermediate level of blocking skill, a more advanced level can be developed through body conditioning. Stationary and moving two-person forearm conditioning drills are used to develop resilience and strength in the arms. At this point, the "block" is often considered as a deflecting strike. The strike occurs with full power using a strengthened arm capable of withstanding the speed and strength of an opponent.

This block represents the classical go-form: a hard technique issued with strength and speed to confront the aggressor. Unfortunately, this hard technique is of little value if the opponent is simply stronger or faster: clearly more is needed.

Transferring Internal Energy

The next stage of development involves the transfer of internal energy into the block from the center of the body. This concept has already been discussed from the viewpoint of transferring internal energy into punching movements in a previous article on Sanchin kata (Labbate, 1999). The idea can also be employed to transfer power directly into the rising block using a shaking motion. To teach this movement, a progressive sequence of drills is used that exaggerate and train the motion of the body. As a student becomes more proficient, these exaggerations gradually decrease until the motion becomes an internal element of the blocking technique.

The preliminary drills focus on the development of the "karate drum" shown in Sequence 2. Standing in a loose ready stance (2A), the student quickly swings the arms and shoulder and clockwise and counterclockwise as far as possible to the right (2B) and left (2C). This swinging motion serves to exaggerate and develop the necessary motion of the hips. A second exercise is then used in which the student drives the swinging action from the hips while holding the arms and body loosely. This latter exercise transitions the student to focus on movement of the hips rather than the shoulders. A third exercise completes the development of the basic turning motion: the hips are driven backward and forward while the shoulders are held in position aligned forward.

Principle #1

The karate drum drills teach the fundamental principles of loading, shaking, locking, and rebounding.

Sanchin style locking is next added to the progression of drills and is shown in Sequence 3: from the ready position (3A), the body is forced through focused tension directly into the locked position (3B). The body becomes firmly rooted to the ground, the body weight is lowered, and each muscle group is brought under tension in a single motion.

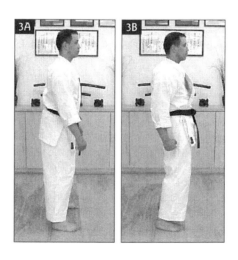

Putting these exercises together, the student can finally develop a complete "karate drum" technique: the hips are driven forward, then allowed naturally to reverberate or rebound back into their final position aligned forward, and finally Sanchin style locking occurs at the close of the technique.

Principle #2

Develop power in the
rising block by directing
internal energy.

After mastering the basic karate drum drills, the student may move forward to drills that cause power to be directed into a particular technique as shown in Sequence 4. In the case of the rising block, this is called an "up–shake." Swinging the arms in the style of the karate drum, the rising block positioning is integrated. For a block with the right arm, the body is rotated as far as possible to the right, the right hand is chambered, and the left arm covers (4A). The shoulders are then rotated, as far to the left (4B) as possible, the left hand remains in the cover position, and the right hand transitions upward in an intercepting motion (4C). The body reverberates back into a final position with the hips aligned forward, the left hand chambers, while the right elbow rotates upward into the block in a redirecting motion until reaching its final position (4D). This cover, intercept, and redirect motion is coordinated and driven from the hips. Sequence 4 exaggerates the body motion to develop the required form, as the student progresses the movements become incrementally smaller until they are an internal aspect of technique.

At the end of this technique, the student applies the locking motion taught as part of the karate drum drills. The student must focus on aligning the hips forward at the end of the block, with the body tightened as in Sanchin kata. Putting these pieces together, the deflecting strike is enhanced to become a powerful strike driven from the hips by internal energy. After the block is complete, the body is locked down as in Sanchin for a split second at the moment of contact when the block completes.

The up-shake is just one of four basic shaking motions that can be applied to all of the basic karate techniques. It can be used to transfer power into any upward movement toward an opponent, for example, rising block, uppercut punch, and elbow strikes. A similar down-shake is used in techniques that move downward into an opponent, for example, down-block, downward strikes and punches. For techniques that involve forward motion of the same hand and leg, such as a lunge punch, palm-heel strike, shuto, etc., an open-shake is used. In contrast, a closed-shake is used for techniques that involve opposite hand and leg movements, for example, a reverse punch, palm-heel strike, etc. Collectively these shaking motions form the principles by which internal energy is transferred into every aspect of structure and movement. These gross movements are practiced only to train the body. Eventually the hips are coordinated with every technique and the associated movement will happen naturally.

Principle #3

Up-, down-, open-, and closed-shakes
allow power to be applied to
every karate technique.

To develop hand-eye coordination, speed, timing, and distancing, the blocks are practiced with a partner. Each level of partner training progressively adds new principles from those listed above, first in stationary, and then in moving drills. In these exercises the timing of the attack is organized by the attacker to be at uneven intervals so that the defender is forced to track and intercept the incoming blow with precision.

Two-Person Sensing Techniques

To make further progress, the advanced student must make a substantive transition to combine the hard techniques of Sanchin with new, soft techniques. The basis of this transition is two-person sensing techniques, a concept that has always been at the center of developing advanced Goju-ryu karate (Higaonna, 1996). The essence of this concept is to make contact with the opponent and retain this contact until the opponent is defeated. In combat, the first point of contact is typically through a block. Having made contact, the opponent's every move can be sensed through feeling so as to maintain control without having to watch his or her movements. This control also makes it possible to confront additional opponents while engaged in combat.

Principle #4

Two-person partner drills, conducted at uneven intervals, are used to develop hand–eye coordination, speed, timing, and distancing.

A number of two-person drills are available to develop this skill. A variety of these drills, that illustrate the basic progression, are explained here to give a feel for the training methods. The drills are cumulative, each building upon the previous to develop and enhance the training process. It is important to practice the drills softly in a relaxed stance. They are intended to develop sensitive, fluid motion rather than force and strength.

Principle #5

Practice two-person sensing techniques slowly and softly to develop the ability to sense and anticipate an opponent's movements without watching.

The first drill is illustrated in Sequence 5 and is concerned with learning to maintain contact by grabbing and sticking. Two students begin in the open-hand middle block position with hands positioned so that a hook is formed at the wrist. The students touch by locking these hooks together (5A). From this grabbing position, both students rotate the hand from outside to inside forming a hook on the opposite side of the wrist (5B). This process is repeated backward and forward. The object of the drill is to develop the sense of sticking to an opponent, grabbing with the hook of the hand, and controlling the contact at all times.

Sequence 6 shows a second drill in which the range of contact is extended to include a palm-heel strike. One partner strikes slowly and carefully (6A) while the other carefully follows the strike inward maintaining light contact at all times. The defender guides the strike to a cupped hand positioned just off the body. The defender then becomes the attacker (6B) and returns the palm-heel while the partner practices the same technique. This drill begins to develop the feeling of following a blow. The attacker determines the speed, power, and direction of the blow while the defender simply focuses on maintaining contact. Through drills of this type, students learn to adhere in the presence of motion and to follow a partner's movement rather than block and lose contact

Sequence 7 shows a drill that is intended to develop the skill of redirecting the energy of an opponent. Like the previous drill, one student uses a palm-heel strike to attack while the other follows the inbound motion to defend and maintain contact. However, at the last moment, prior to the strike making contact, the defender redirects the blow by rotating the hips away causing the blow to miss the body entirely (7A), following which the roles of defender and attacker are reversed (7B). This is more difficult than the previous drills in that it requires the attacker not to overcommit and the defender to sense when the attack has terminated in order to begin a return attack. Through gentle soft motions it is possible to develop a sense for redirecting the opponent's energy away from the body and loading the internal energy into the body. Notice that the basic hook developed in the first drill is used to control the direction when redirecting the incoming blow.

Sequence 8 illustrates a final drill bringing together the skills of sticking, sensing, loading, redirecting, and rebounding. As before, the drill begins with a palm-heel strike by the attacker (8A) in which the defender sticks and follows (8B). The strike is then blocked, loading energy for a counter while redirecting the opponents energy (8C). Finally, the defender counters with a palm-heel strike (8D).

The principles of sensing, sticking, and redirecting are now used in all of the standard partner training drills. However, these drills are utilized to focus on maintaining contact rather than delivering the appropriate sequence of blocks and blows. Sequence 9 shows a blocking drill conducted in this manner. First the students practice these drills with their eyes open, then with their eyes closed. The object is to maintain contact at all times, anticipating the opponent's movements by sensing the position of their body. The drill begins from the ready stance (9A). In this case, the initial attacker is on the left side of the photo. The attacker strikes to the face and the defender makes initial contact through a rising block (9B). The defender then counters to the body and the attacker senses this movement. The attacker maintains contact, feeling the motion of the defender to intercept the incoming blow. At the point of interception the attacker is touching in two places (9C), allowing the point of contact to move to the new block and allowing the right hand to be chambered while maintaining contact (9D). After this attack to the body, the attacker strikes to the groin (9E), and is in turn blocked by the defender who maintains contact (9F). Roles then reverse with the defender striking to the face.

Principle #6

Practice two-person sensing techniques in blocking drills with a partner with the eyes closed to develop the senses.

In combat, we seek to maintain contact at all times so as to read the opponent with our senses. When contact is lost it is generally a cue to attack since the opponent is repositioning to attempt some alternative technique.

Principle #7

Use body-shifting to allow a blow to pass and reposition the body to advantage.

Body-Shifting

Body-shifting (*taisabaki*) is a technique in which the goal is to move in relation to the attacker both to avoid a blow and gain a position of advantage (Okazaki & Stricevic, 1984). The simplest form of this concept is termed "opening the door." If the defender is standing in a ready stance, and the attacker attempts to strike with the left hand, the defender moves the right foot backward, rotating the body by 90-degrees to avoid the blow. This technique places the defender on the inside and in position to counter. A similar technique with the right foot can be used to avoid a left forward punch. Although this technique is simple, it is preferable to position the body to the outside of the attacker where there is less likelihood that the attacker will be able to use a second technique.

Body-shifting movements can be achieved on any angle, not simply backward. For example, Sequence 10 shows how to combine the technique with the rising block. The attacker attempts a right-punch, the defender intercepts and adheres to the blow, moving to the left on a 45-degree line with the left foot, while maintaining contact and following the opponent (10A). The right foot is then positioned so that the defender is in an advantageous position, on the outside of the attacker, with the groin protected from kicks 10B). During this movement, the rising block is used to expose the ribs by grabbing with the muscular part of the forearm. Body-shifting ensures the correct distancing to effect the counter (10C). Irrespective of the stance in use, when moving to the left, the left foot moves first followed by the right; when moving to the right, the right foot moves first followed by the left.

It is important to overcome the student's natural tendency to step back during the delivery of a blocking technique. Stepping backward is useful as a teaching tool when students are learning the basic gross patterns of blocking as it prevents their inadvertently being hurt. At more advanced levels it produces a defensive mind-set and represents an error in conditioning that places the student at a distinct disadvantage by causing loss of contact. This in turn prevents the ability to sense and control the opponent's movements. Movement to the side, as shown above, is a common alternative and is a distinct improvement as it allows sensitivity techniques to be used.

Advanced Level Block

Combining the transfer of internal energy with sensitivity techniques and body-shifting, students can at last progress to more advanced level blocking techniques. The advanced level block is shown exaggerated in Sequence 11 to highlight the main ideas. Although these photos show stationary poses, it is important to recognize that the entire photo sequence is performed as one fluid motion.

Instead of blocking from the chamber at 45-degrees in a deflecting motion, the block is positioned first to intercept the incoming blow as shown in photo 11A. This occurs at the earliest point the chambered hand can reach the incoming blow and takes the shortest path to interception. The position of the interception is almost vertical and occurs with the muscular part of the forearm. It provides the first point of contact and the defender immediately adheres to the opponent. The motion of the arm continues upward in a circular motion redirecting the opponent's energy (11B). The defender's arm then rotates into its final position pulling the opponent's arm out of danger by adhering and redirecting at the point of contact (11C). No force is required to achieve this block irrespective of the power and speed of the incoming blow. It occurs as a light, effortless, and fluid motion maintaining contact at all times.

As the block begins to redirect the blow, notice that the defender's hips are back, loaded, as shown in photo 11C. As the defender redirects the opponent's energy with the block, he steps straight in and strikes with a counter punch using the additional power generated from turning the waist (11D). This strike occurs with the full force of the loaded energy. The defender remains in contact at all times even though striking a blow. The counter strike occurs before the opponent has time to form a subsequent attack. Following the counter-strike the defender is reloaded in the opposite direction with both hands in contact. A wide variety of follow-through attacks can now be achieved while remaining in contact with either hand.

Principle #9

Intercept, stick, redirect, lock, counter, and reload in single fluid motion.

TECHNICAL SECTION

We have so far considered the rising block as a deflecting technique, as a powerful strike, and as a method for redirecting an opponent's energy. However, the technique can be used in wide variety of applications. A few of these are demonstrated here to give a flavor for the more general utility of the technique.

Grappling Techniques

At close quarters the block is useful in obtaining space. For example, in Sequence 12 the attacker is grappling close in and in order to use any techniques the defender must create some space (12A). The defender first grabs the attacker (12B) and strikes to the forearm to loosen the opponent's hold. Then the opponent's pushed away using the "block" (12C). While remaining in contact to read the opponent's movements, multiple strikes can then be made.

Typical grabs, such as that shown in Sequence 13, can also be confronted using the block. In these applications, the chambered hand is always used to trap and control the opponent. For example, in Sequence 13 the attacker grabs the defender (13A) who immediately clasps the grabbing hand (13B). Holding the grab in place, a block is used downward to soften the opponent's arm and pull him forward (13C). At the same time, the wrist is turned downward causing the opponent to be sucked into a subsequent strike to the neck (13D). Notice that after initial contact is made (13B), the defender never looses contact until the attacker is defeated.

The technique can be used in other grappling positions, such as that shown in photo 14A. Here the defender steps backward and holds the attacker's head downward (14B). This provides direct access for a downward strike to the nape of the neck (14C). Again, after initial contact, the defender remains in contact until satisfied that the attacker is defeated.

Penetration Punch

Sequence 15 shows the use of the "block" as a penetration punch. Initial contact occurs during the block where the attacker expects a standard block (15A), instead, the blocking arm rotates upward fully, striking the attacker in the temple (15B, 15C). Notice that contact is maintained throughout the technique. The defender keeps the attacker's arm under control while delivering the punch. The attacker's own energy is used to drive the defender's strike in at the temple.

Choke

Sequence 16 shows how to use the "block" to enter a choke. The application begins with the attacker pushing (16A). The defender then traps downward to obtain contact (16B). While maintaining contact, a rising block is then performed directly to the neck (16C). The opposite hand is then moved under the blocking arm to grab the opposite collar (16D). The knuckles on the blocking hand are then forced upward into the opponent's neck by pulling the opposite hand downward at the same time as forcing the blocking hand upward (16E). Tight contact is maintained through the blocking arm at all times leading to strangulation (16F).

Principle #10

A "block" is multi-role technique that can
be used in a wide variety of applications
that include grappling, striking, choking,
take-downs, as well as blocking.

Take Down

The block can also be used as part of a take-down. For example, in photo 17A, the
attacker ducks to avoid a blow and grabs at the ankle while striking to the hip
joint. The take-down is affected by striking with the "block" (17B) while pulling
at the ankle until the opponent falls (17C).

The applications presented here are
by no means exhaustive. They simply
represent a cross-section of representative uses for the rising block alone.

Concluding Remarks

The Goju-ryu principles presented at the beginner level provide simple basic forms that were never intended to guide the practitioner in applications. They are primarily learning tools to progress along the path to advanced technique. Most of these basic ideas can be used in a multitude of applications in combat. However, to be useful they must be based on the principles of structure, movement, and breathing developed through Sanchin kata. Subsequently, advanced principles must be added: transferring internal energy into every technique, sensing skills to intercept, adhere, and redirect an opponent's energy, and body-shifting to position the body. Correct distancing, timing, and hand–eye coordination must be developed progressively through stationary and moving partner training. As overall technique improves, the quality and subtlety of kata training grows to incorporate more advanced movements. Thus each incremental improvement is fed back into every aspect of progressive training. Finally, applications evolve not as a staged set of movements, but rather as an artistic combination of the practitioner's ideas and training. Karate is then no longer concerned with mastering a technique. In the end it is concerned with mastering oneself.

References

Higaonna, M. (1996). *The history of karate*. Norwich, UK: Dragon Books.

Labbate, M. (1999). Elements of advanced karate techniques. *Journal of Asian Martial Arts, 8*(2), 80–95.

Okazaki, T., & Stricevic, M. (1984). *The textbook of modem karate*. Tokyo: Kodansha International.

Oyama, M. (1981). *Mastering karate*. New York: Grosset & Dunlap.

Tensho Kata:
Goju-Ryu's Secret Treasure

by Marvin Labbate

All photos courtesy of M. Labbate.

Introduction

This chapter is the third in a series of writings that examines the fundamental principles of Goju-Ryu karate. The first chapter discussed the style's hard (*go*) elements: the external principles of structure, movement, and breathing developed through the study of the Sanchin kata (Labbate, 1999). These principles are generally the focus of attention during the first three years of study and are the foundation on which all other aspects of karate are built. The second chapter focused on transitional principles, such as the karate drum, push-hands, body shifting, and partner training (Labbate, 2000). These concepts were introduced through the study of the rising block and are typically taught in the two years prior to reaching black-belt level. This chapter describes some soft (*ju*) principles of Goju-Ryu developed through the study of the Tensho kata. The origin of these principles is undoubtedly Chinese and Master Miyagi Chojun clearly intended them to be taught only after the Sanchin principles were mastered.

One of the most subtle and beautiful movement series in the style, Tensho is the internal kata of structure and movement and is typically taught as the first kata beyond 1st-dan black-belt level. The kata builds upon all of the concepts presented in the previous chapters and adds principles of soft fluid motion, weight transitioning, connectivity, and opening and closing. These new principles are illustrated here through the study of two of the opening sequences from the kata. Taken alone, Tensho is deceptively simple and beautiful, but beneath it is hidden a wealth of martial treasure.

Tensho Basics

Tensho should initially be performed as a hard kata, using the basic principles taught through the study of the Sanchin kata. These principles induce body tension, build strength, and ensure the correct positioning of muscle groups, especially the shoulder muscle group. To illustrate this relationship, Sequences 1 and 2 show two of the crucial opening sequences from Tensho. The first sequence begins from the double block position in right Sanchin stance (1A). As the left hand is placed into the chambered position, the right hand is opened (1B). The right hand is then turned over into a hooking block position (1C). From this position, a knife-hand (*shuto*) block is performed (1D), and the right hand is brought to the chamber position (1E). Finally, the right hand is used to perform a palm-heel strike to the head (1F).

The second sequence shown follows directly in the kata. After the palm-heel strike (2A), the right hand is rotated downward (2B), and then drawn inward to the chamber position (2C). Finally, a second palm-heel strike occurs (2D). These sequences are repeated later in the kata on the left, in a left Sanchin stance.

Notice how all of the principles of structure, movement, and breathing are carried over from Sanchin kata. The entire shoulder muscle group acts as a single structure under tension, and is locked down at the end of each motion. Tension is induced through correct positioning of the hand, arm, and elbow. The shoulders remain down and aligned forward. Sanchin stance is used to bring all of the leg muscles under tension; the body weight is lowered and becomes firmly rooted, gripping the floor through correct positioning of the feet. Breathing is coordinated with movement, following the general guidelines used in lifting weights: breath is inhaled during preparatory movements such as a block or counter; it is expelled during exertions such as striking motions. Thus in Sequence 1, the entire sequence from (1A) up to and including (1E) is used to inhale, and only the strike (1F) is associated with exhalation. In Sequence 2, the entire sequence from (2A) through (2C) is used to inhale; the final strike (2D) is coordinated with the exhale. Finally, to develop power in the techniques, transitional principles such as the karate drum can be integrated with kata training (Labbate, 2000).

Practice Tensho softly and fluidly, maintaining
muscles relaxed externally, and firm internally.

Soft Fluid Motion

While Sanchin-style practice develops the general form associated with the kata, it fails significantly to develop power in the techniques. The next stage of development requires a radical change to incorporate soft (*ju*) principles into training. The essence of the concept is to practice the kata using continuous, soft, fluid motion. Soft practice should be combined with exercises to develop internal ki energy. The goal is to develop the ability to hold muscles relaxed externally, providing fluidity, yet firm internally, providing strength. The entire sequence in number one is practiced as a single movement without breaks between the techniques. Similarly, the entire sequence in number two is a single movement.

To understand this internal principle, place the arm into the position shown in Sequence 3 (A) with a partner (on the left) supporting the arm. If the arm is relaxed, the partner feels the heaviness of the arm as it fails to support itself; if the arm is released it falls away without control (3B). If instead the arm is held using the principles of Sanchin kata, the shoulder muscle group is locked down, the arm is held under (3C). The partner feels no weight and the arm remains in position when released. Now the concepts from both these extremes are merged: externally, the arm is correctly positioned and supports it own weight, yet there is no tension or strain; internally the arm is relaxed and flexible, able to move with fluidity, speed, and strength.

When Tensho is practiced in this soft, fluid manner, attention must be paid to the tempo of the movements: each movement on the left is balanced in time with the corresponding movement on the right. Every pause on the left should correspond with a pause of the same duration on the right. Attention to tempo in this manner ensures that techniques can be performed with the same proficiency on both sides of the body.

PRINCIPLE #2

Every kata has an associated tempo and timing. Movements on the
left must be balanced carefully with those on the right.

Building upon this soft form of kata training, it is now possible to show the push-hands (*kakie*) applications derived from Tensho: principles that allow a defender to sense and anticipate an opponent's movements (Labbate, 2000). First consider the kata's opening movement shown in Sequence 4 (A) in which the right hand is opened. This corresponds directly to the opening on-guard position of all kakie drills as shown in 4B. This position teaches students to use a hook formed at the wrist to grab and hold an opponent.

In the next movement from the kata, shown in Sequence 5 (A–C), the right hand begins in the on-guard position, turns over to grab with a hooking block (5B), and finally performs a knife-hand block (5C). This corresponds to the first push-hands drill that teaches grabbing and sticking. Two students begin in the on-guard position with hands positioned so that a grab is formed at the wrist; the students touch by locking these hooks together (5D). From this grabbing position, both students roll theirs hands over at the wrist maintaining contact (5E). Finally, they rotate their hands from outside to inside, maintaining contact so as to form a hook on the opposite side of the wrist (5F). This process is repeated backward and forward to develop the sense of grabbing with the hook of the hand, sticking to an opponent, and controlling contact at all times.

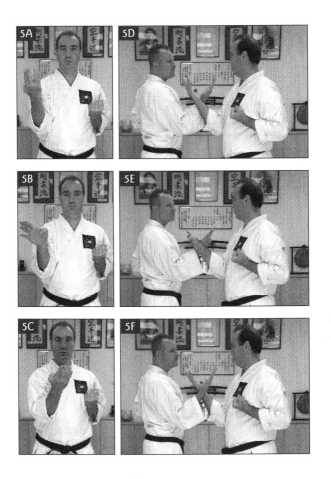

Sequence 6 shows the next sequence from the kata in which the right hand performs a knife-hand block (6A), is brought to the chambered position (6B), and then used for a palm-heel strike (6C).

This movement corresponds to the second push-hands drill, shown in Sequence 7. As in previous push-hands drills, this movement begins in the on-guard position (7A). The attacker then strikes slowly and carefully while the defender follows the strike inward maintaining light contact at all times (7B). The defender guides the strike to a cupped-hand positioned just off the body. The defender then becomes the attacker and returns the palm-heel strike while the partner practices the same technique (7D). This drill begins to develop the feeling of following an attack. The attacker determines the strike's speed, power, and direction while the defender simply focuses on maintaining contact. Through drills of this type, students learn to adhere in the presence of motion and to follow a partner's movement rather than block and lose contact.

The same movement from the kata can also be applied through a third push-hands drill, shown in Sequence 8, to develop the skill of redirecting the energy of an opponent. Again, the movement begins from the on-guard position (8A). One student then uses a palm-heel strike to attack, which the other follows and maintains contact. However, just before contact, the defender redirects the strike by rotating the hips away, causing the strike to miss the body entirely (8B). The roles are then reversed and the attacker redirects (8C). Once again the basic hook is used to grab and stick to the attacker.

PRINCIPLE #3

Push-hands corresponds to the application of the Tensho kata and teaches sticking, sensing, following, redirecting, loading, and rebounding (countering).

Recall now the second segment from the kata, shown again for clarity in Sequence 9 (A–D). This segment teaches the fourth push-hands drill that brings together the several soft skills: grabbing, sticking, following, redirecting, loading, and rebounding (countering). The drill begins with the grabbing position (9E). The attacker then performs a palm-heel strike to which the defender sticks and follows (9F). The strike is blocked, redirecting the opponent's energy while loading energy for a counter (9G). Roles are then reversed allowing the attacker to stick, redirect, load (9H), and counter (9I).

Weight Transitioning

The karate drum refers to a series of drills that gradually teach the student the internal structure associated with delivering power in karate techniques (Labbate, 2000). These concepts are natural to employ in the further development of Tensho kata. For example, the sequence numbers one and two are used to load energy that can subsequently be used during an associated palm-heel strike.

Building upon these procedures, a new principle can now be added to place weight behind the delivery of each technique and enhance stability. The central concept is to transfer weight between techniques so that the body is always in either an offensive or defensive posture; rooted to the floor, at the same time stable and balanced. Sequence 10 shows a simple drill that builds upon the karate drum to develop this principle. The karate drum technique is practiced from a right Sanchin stance. However, as the right hip and shoulder swing forward, weight is transferred to the forward foot (10A), as the right hip and shoulder transition backward, weight is transferred to the backward foot (10B). The general weight distribution is approximately 70% to 30% to ensure stability. Notice that the motion of the arms follow the hips' rotation, and the body sinks as it moves backward to accept the additional weight on the rear leg (10B).

There are several common errors to be avoided in performing this drill. When swinging forward and backward, the student should not lean excessively into the drill, the shoulders should rotate remaining parallel to the floor, and the student should not tip from side to side. Many of the common errors can be avoided by slow practice with the knees slightly bent.

Centering and Connectivity

Previous chapters have explained in depth that power does not originate in the movements of the arm during a punch or strike. Instead, it emanates from the center of the body, and in particular the *tanden*, a region in the lower abdomen (Labbate, 1999: 87). Many of the drills described in these chapters are concerned with how incrementally to build techniques that transfer this energy into the powerful delivery of blocks, punches, and kicks (Labbate, 2000).

In combat, motion costs time and it is important to deliver techniques with the strong solid muscular position of Sanchin in a manner directly connected to the center of energy in the body and without extraneous movements. The practice of Tensho is now used to build these centering and connectivity concepts as shown in Sequence 11. These movements are taken from the first Tensho sequence (1C–D). In the open-hand middle block position, a fist is placed between the elbow and the rib cage (11A). In performing the knife-hand block (11B), the arm is kept connected to the center of the body as the block is performed and the shoulder muscle group maintains Sanchin structure. Notice that the only manner in which this transition can occur is when the body rotates from the center into the knife-hand block. All of the techniques in Tensho can be practiced in this manner, maintaining Sanchin structure.

PRINCIPLE #4

Weight transitioning is used to reinforce
the transfer of power into a technique
and enhance stability.

Sequence 12 shows how this technique is combined with weight transition-ing. As the hooking block is performed, weight transitions to the rear, catching, grabbing, and redirecting a blow (12A). As the knife-hand block is performed, weight transfers to the forward foot delivering power into the block (12B).

PRINCIPLE #5

Connectivity and centering are
used at close-quarters to ensure
that energy is delivered directly with Sanchin
structure without extraneous motion.

Opening and Closing

Although Sanchin structure is important in all aspects of training for main-taining the correct positioning of muscle groups, it lacks a key ingredient used in transferring power into a strike. The desired outcome is an explosion of energy directed at a point on the opponent's body. Unfortunately, at this final moment of contact, Sanchin's hard structure inhibits the flow of energy. An analogy that is helpful in understanding this difference is to think of the destructive force of a whip: the whip is drawn loosely back to load energy and then flicked at great speed so that the tip strikes for an instant and is then retracted immediately. The blow is extremely painful because of the tremendous kinetic energy built in the whip and transferred to a single point of impact. The alternative is a soft principle in which a strike opens to transfer energy and closes to load energy for the next technique, just like the whip in the analogy. This concept is illustrated through the palm-heel strike taken from Tensho in Sequence 13. The strike is delivered from the chambered position (13A). Sanchin structure is momentarily lost as the shoulder muscle group is opened allowing energy to flow from the center into the strike (13B). After the strike has made impact, the shoulder muscle group returns to a locked Sanchin structure, conserving the remaining energy for the next technique (13C).

PRINCIPLE #6
Opening and closing
provides an explosive release
of energy directed
at the instant of a strike.

Putting all of the concepts together, let us now reexamine the opening sequence of the Tensho kata taken from Sequence 1. Sequence 14 (A–E) shows the new soft fluid movement; notice how different the sequence is from the hard original structure. The first open-hand middle block is combined with weight transitioning (14A) to grab and redirect the opponent. Movement to the second knife-hand block is achieved without extraneous arm motion, maintaining Sanchin structure by weight transitioning and moving from the center (14B). Energy is then loaded into the palm-heel strike (14C) and delivered by opening and closing to transfer energy into the strike (14D). Notice the position of the hand when preparing the palm-heel strike (14C), just like a whip being wound up and flicked into the opponent. The transition from this position to the final strike position occurs gradually throughout the technique, just as a whip unravels during flight.

Sequences 15 and 16 demonstrate the difference between the conventional Sanchin structure for the palm-heel strike and the modified structure based on the combination of these new principles. Although powerful and hard, the Sanchin style strike in Sequence 15 has only a moderate effect on the glove representing the opponent (15B). In contrast, the modified strike loads energy like the whip (16A), smoothly transitions the energy into the strike (16C), explodes with devastating impact upon the target (16D), and subsequently returns to a locked Sanchin structure in preparation for subsequent movements (16E). Notice the synchronization of body and strike, reminiscent of the whip that lunges power at the opponent while supporting the strike with the appropriate structure.

Applications

Sequence 17 demonstrates the practical application of the first sequence from Tensho shown in Sequence 1. An initial punch from the attacker is immediately blocked with an open-hand block (17A). At this point, contact has been made with the attacker (push-hands), allowing his/her movements to be determined by sensing while the first strike is redirected away from the defender. An immediate second punch by the attacker is then intercepted using a knife-hand block with the same hand (17B). This block redirects the opponent while loading energy (17C) for the final palm-heel strike (17D). The shoulder muscle group then returns to a locked Sanchin structure (17E). The entire sequence is carried out as a single movement, without breaks between the techniques. Its circular style effectively winds up energy in the body that is deposited onto the attacker's chin at the end of the sequence. Notice the use of weight transitioning correctly to position and support the movements throughout this sequence.

Sequence 18 shows a practical close-in application of the second sequence from Tensho. Here the defender grabs an incoming strike (18A), sticks to the opponent, and redirects the strike (18B). Energy is loaded by the defender (18C) and then transferred into the opponent with a strike to the groin (18D). Notice how weight transitioning is used to position the body (18C) for this technique, and power is transferred by opening and closing (18D).

Conclusion

Goju-Ryu is a close-in fighting style that couples soft principles, for sensing and anticipating the movements of an opponent, with internal methods for transferring power at close quarters. The Tensho kata contains Okinawan push-hands drills (*kakie*) and incorporates a wealth of concealed meanings to teach and develop the style's soft internal components. The kata builds upon Sanchin, the external kata of structure, movement, and breathing, together with transitional techniques such as the karate drum. Soft fluid motion is then used to couple speed and power; weight transitioning maintains stability when redirecting an opponent and reinforcing subsequent counters. Moving from the center reduces extraneous arm movement and maintains a reinforced structure. Finally, opening and closing provides explosive force at the point of impact. These concepts are but a few of the kata's hidden treasures. Others, beyond the scope of this paper, include shedding as a method of forcing an opponent to lose balance and structure, trapping to immobilize an attack, folding to refine a succession of blows, and multi-strike timing to ensure that counterattacks strike an opponent between breaths.

In Goju-Ryu, beginning students find comprehension of elements that are fundamentally hard (*go*) and external easiest to accomplish. The study of soft (*ju*) and internal elements must build upon that foundation. At that point, understanding of the meaning of the pairings of hard-soft and external-internal principles becomes possible. For this objective, there is no better vehicle of study than Tensho. The relatively simple and beautiful structure of this complex kata is indeed deceptive.

Bibliography

Labbate, M. (1999). Elements of advanced karate techniques. *Journal of Asian Martial Arts*, 8(2), 80–95.

Labbate, M. (2000). Developing advanced Goju-Ryu techniques. *Journal of Asian Martial Arts*, 9(1), 56–69.

Acknowledgment

Special thanks to 2nd-dan Gregory Scheureer for assisting in the technical sequences, and to Steven Taylor for taking the photographs.

An Analysis of Parallel Techniques: The Kinetic Connection Between Sanseru & Shishochin

by Robert Toth

All photographs by Wai Hung Tang.

Introduction

Is there a secret connection between the traditional Goju-Ryu routines (*kata*) called Sanseru and Shishochin? Has something been hidden from practitioners regarding them? Perhaps the key to understanding them better lies in the routines themselves. The purpose of this article is to look at the technical relationship between these two. The templates of both routines are very similar.

History

The founder of Goju-Ryu, Miyagi Chojun, was born in Naha, Okinawa, on April 25, 1888. His family imported pharmaceuticals and was one of the wealthiest in Naha (Porta & McCabe, 1994: 64; Higaonna, 1985: 25). Miyagi began his martial arts training with Aragaki Ryuko when he was eleven years old. Three years later, Aragaki introduced his student to Higaonna Kanryo. As a youth, Higaonna had studied martial arts with Aragaki Seisho and Kojo Taitei (Hokama, 1998: 36). Higaonna had also spent a number of years in Fuzhou, China, studying the martial arts with Ryu Ryu Ko (McCarthy, 1987: 30; Higaonna 1985: 22). Higaonna Kanryo's style has been called Nahate. Miyagi Chojun trained with Higaonna Kanryo until Higaonna's death in 1916. In that year, Miyagi also made his first trip to China to further his martial arts knowledge.

Miyagi Chojun used twelve routines (*kata*) as part of his training syllabus: Sanchin, Gekisai I, Gekisai II, Saifa, Shishochin, Sanseru, Seiunchin, Sesan, Sepai, Kururunfa, Suparimpei, and Tensho (Porta & McCabe, 1994: 66). Of these, Miyagi was involved in the creation of four. Miyagi and Nagamine Shoshin created Gekisai I in 1940; Nagamine called it Fukyugata (Nagamine, 1976: 104; Sells, 2000: 227-228). Miyagi alone created Gekisai II. Miyagi revised the breathing exercise Sanchin that Higaonna Kanryo taught him. And the routine considered his masterpiece, Tensho, was based on the Rokkishu (Higaonna, 1985: 26), which is found in the old Chinese martial arts text, *Bubishi* (McKenna, 2000: 38). It is believed that the other Goju-Ryu routines were passed down from Higaonna Kanryo, who had learned them from Ryu Ryu Ko in Fuzhou, China (Higaonna, 1986: 15).

In 1885, Higaonna Kanryo brought Sanseru from Fuzhou (Sells, 2000: 275), but its lineage after that is uncertain. In the postscript of the translation of Miyagi's "Outline of Karate-do," Kinjo Hiroshi states, "...the fighting tradition established by master Miyagi was based upon the southern kung-fu [gongfu] style which his teacher Higaonna Kanryo had brought from Fuzhou..." (Miyagi, 1934: 26).

There is some question as to whether Miyagi learned Sanseru from Higaonna. It seems that Higaonna taught Sanseru to Kyoda Juhatsu, his senior student, but not to Miyagi (McKenna, 2000: 39, 42). Miyagi learned a different version elsewhere, possibly during one of his trips to China or from an Okinawan source other than Higaonna.

Some historians also believe that Higaonna brought Shishochin back from China (Sells, 2000: 274). But Richard Kim, in his article "Shorinji ryu: An overview of all karate kata" and in one of his lectures at Guelph University, Ontario, Canada, says that only the Goju-Ryu students of Miyagi train in Shishochin (Kim, 1992: 15).

If Miyagi Chojun did not learn Sanseru from Higaonna, then he might not have learned Shishochin from him either. Either both routines came from the same source (other than Higaonna), or Miyagi Chojun created Shishochin after learning Sanseru from that other source.

Over the years, the personal students of Miyagi Chojun have said little about their teacher and his teacher before him. Perhaps they also followed the attitude of Kanzaki Shigekazu, one of Kyoda Juhatsu's students, who thought that it was impolite to ask questions about Higaonna Kanryo (McKenna, 2000: 54).

Miyagi Chojun, the only man who knew the origins of the Goju-Ryu routines stated, "The only detail we can be sure of is that during the eleventh year of Bunsei [1828] a Chinese system from Fuzhou unfurled and was studied deeply, and from which goju ryu karate kempo ascended" (Miyagi, 1934: 21).[1] With Miyagi's death in 1953, the origins of the Goju-Ryu kata, and especially the relationship between Sanseru and Shishochin, will never be certain.

Comparing Techniques from Shishochin and Sanseru

Higaonna Morio has said that Shishochin was a favorite routine of Miyagi Chojun in his latter years (1986: 113). Shishochin means "Four Directional Battle" and concentrates on four-directional fighting, consisting of open-hand strikes: spear-hand and palm strikes (Yagi, 2000: 82).

Sanseru uses very strong attacking techniques. Written in Chinese characters, Sanseru means the number "36."

The theme of the two routines is the same at the beginning. Both Shishochin and Sanseru start with three steps forward in an hour-glass stance (*sanchin dachi*).

1A: Sanseru—
uses closed fists.
1B: Shishochin—
uses open hand strikes.

2A–B: Sanseru—
a technique to
release from a
hand grab.

3A–B:
Shishochin—
a technique
to release from
a choke.

4: Sanseru—
attacking an
opponent's knee.

5: Shishochin—
attacking an
opponent's elbow.

The next two Shishochin movements are not connected to the Sanseru routine, but they do not negate this chapter's premise. The Shishochin elbow attack is repeated on the left side using the left forearm. Then Shishochin brings the feet together and attacks with the right elbow (or punches over the shoulder, depending on the interpretation).

Now the routines work against each other. While Sanseru kicks north, Shishochin blocks and strikes south (6). Then Sanseru kicks south, and Shishochin blocks and strikes north. Sanseru turns and kicks east; Shishochin blocks and strikes west. Then, Sanseru kicks west, and Shishochin blocks and strikes east. If you could overlay diagrams of the Sanseru and Shishochin movements, and view them from above, you can see the connection.

6

The next two movements are not in a complementary sequence, but are consistent as far as their application. After Sanseru's fourth front kick, the practitioner shifts into a modified horse stance (*shiko dachi*) with the hands crossed and down, facing south. The application of this movement could be a wrist grab against Shishochin's move facing north (7). Then, Shishochin's reaction to Sanseru's wrist grab is to pull the hand up and hit with the elbow (8). Sanseru's next movement is a lapel grab facing north in a horse stance (9). Shishochin then steps into a cat stance (*neko ashi dachi*) facing south, breaks the grip, and steps in doing a head butt (10).

7–8: Shishochin's release and counter
against Sanseru's double hand grab.

9–10: Shishochin's release from a lapel
grab and the head butt counter.

Shishochin then kicks to the east. Sanseru responds by grabbing the kicking leg (11A) and sweeping Shishochin's support leg to complete the throw (11B). Shishochin kicks again, and Sanseru counter with the same throw. Again, if you overlay these movements and view them from above, you can see the connection.

The two movements before the final movement of Shishochin are supplementary in that they are not connected to Sanseru, but serve to balance the routine. They do not affect the premise of this chapte. These movements are two more elbow breaks: one with the left forearm and one with the right, both facing south; then stepping into *musuba dachi* (heels together, toes apart) with a left elbow (or punch over the shoulder), again facing south.

The last technique in both Sanseru and Shishochin are throws (12–13).

Conclusion

Sanseru and Shishochin relate in two ways. First, we see that parts of one routine act as the application of the other. At some point perhaps that is what Shishochin was: a drill to practice some of the applications of Sanseru. Shishochin has also been supplemented with movements—such as the releases, joint attacks, and takedowns—at the beginning and end that are similar in theme to Sanseru. The similarities in Sanseru and Shishochin substantiate the idea that these two Goju-Ryu routines are related.[2]

Notes

[1] Perhaps Miyagi was referring to Sakiyama Kitoku and Nakaima Kenri, both from Naha, Okinawa, who may have trained in China before Higaonna Kanryo (Sells, 2000: 43).

[2] One of Miyagi Chojun's senior students, Yagi Meitoku, has created five additional routines. Tenshi can be split into two forms that work against each other; one is the application of the other. The pairs Byakko and Seiryu and Genbu and Shujakku work in the same way. Perhaps Miyagi also passed down the idea of one form holding the applications of another.

Bibliography

Higaonna, M. (1985). *Traditional karate do Okinawa Goju-Ryu, Vol. 1*. Toyko: Minato Research and Publishing Co.

Higaonna, M. (1986). *Traditional karate do Okinawa Goju-Ryu Vol. 2*. Toyko: Minato Research and Publishing Co.

Hokama, T. & Borkowski, C. (Trans.) (1998). *History and traditions of Okinawan karate*. Hamilton, Ontario: Masters Publication.

Kim, R. (1992, Fall). Shorinji ryu: An overview of all kata forms. *Budo Dojo:* 13–16.

McCarthy, P. (1987). *Classical kata of Okinawan karate*. Santa Clarita, CA: Ohara Publications.

McCarthy, P. (1995). *The bible of karate, Bubishi*. Rutland, VT: Tuttle.

McKenna, M. (2000), To'on-ryu: A glimpse into karate-do's roots. *Journal of Asian Martial Arts*, 9(3), 32–43.

McKenna, M. (2000) Kanzaki Shigekazu: An interview with To'on-ryu's leading representative. *Journal of Asian Martial Arts*, 9(3), 45–57.

Miyagi, C., & International Ryukyu Karate Research Society (Trans.) (1934). *Karate-doh Gaisetsu: An outline of karate-doh*. Yokohama, Japan: International Ryukyu Karate Research Society.

Nagamine, S. (1976). *The essesnce of Okinawan karate do*. Rutland, VT: Tuttle.

Porta, J., & McCabe, J. (1994). The karate of Chojun Miyagi. *Journal of Asian Martial Arts, 3*(3), 62–71.

Sells, J. (2000). *Unante: The secrets of karate*. Hollywood, CA: W.M. Hawley.

Yagi, M. (2000). *Okinawan karate do Goju-Ryu Meibukan*. Dundas, Ontario: Yagi-Wheeler-Vickerson, L.T. Designs Ltd.

Acknowledgment

A special thanks goes to Corey Belliveau, Carry Smith, and Lawrence Macoretta for appearing in the photos; to Wai Hung Tang for taking the photos; to Olga Toth for setting up the photos and to Lisa Toth and Cam McGill for proof reading the article. Great appreciation also goes to Sensei Richard Kim for his guidance.

Incorporating the Main Principles of Kata Training

by Marvin Labbate

All photos courtesy of M. Labbate.

Introduction

This is the fourth in a series of chapters that describe the core principals of Okinawan Goju-Ryu karatedo. Previous articles focused on hard principles of structure, movement, and breathing (Labbate, 1999); intermediate principals associated with building, controlling, and transferring internal energy (Labbate, 2000); and soft principals associated with making contact, following, and controlling an opponent (Labbate, 2001). This article builds upon these ideas and incorporates them into a general set of kata training principals. Kata are stylized fighting forms, or sequences, developed over the centuries and based on actual combat experience. Here the ideas are illustrated through the study of Kata Seiunchin. However, each Goju-Ryu kata can be developed with the same ideas.

Every kata exists at many levels of sophistication and can be studied from a broad variety of viewpoints. At the most basic level, a kata is simply a pattern of movements that train typical fighting scenarios. At the most advanced level, a kata is a sequence of dangerous vital point strikes that can cause paralysis, unconsciousness, or death. Between these extremes are levels of development to which the masters of old tightly controlled access. The highest levels were transmitted orally to only a chosen son, or in the absence of a son, to a top student. This control was not simply to provide an advantage in combat: it provided safeguards to ensure that the information was transmitted to only those who proved to be of the appropriate spiritual and moral background, people who would exercise social responsibility in their teaching and use of the ideas. In modern times, these controls have been sadly undermined for commercial gain. A number of books and seminars have appeared that teach extremely dangerous techniques without integrity or an appreciation of the concepts' medical implications. This article takes some techniques from the Seiunchin kata that have recently become well known, and explores their devastating significance to underlie the importance of responsible teaching methods.

Basic Kata Training

At its heart, every kata contains a sequence of basic moves that must be memorized by the student. For example, the opening movements of Seiunchin are shown in Figure 1. Initially, the right foot moves forward 45 degrees into a straddle-leg stance (*shiko dachi*) and both hands are chambered (1A). Once in shiko dachi, both hands move straight up simultaneously to a spear-hand strike (*morote sukui uke*) and are placed back-to-back as they reach chin level (1B); the elbows in this position should be about a fist distance from the ribs, the fingertips are at chin height and are pointed upwards. Remaining in the straddle-leg stance, both hands then perform an augmented downward block (*morote gedan uke*) (1C). Both hands then make a right upward scooping block (*sukui uke*), the right hand palm faces upwards while performing the block while the left hand moves into an open handed chambered position (1D). While keeping the left hand chambered, a right hand hooking block (*kaki uke*) is then performed (1E). Finally, the left hand performs a finger thrust (*hira nukite tsuki*) as the right hand draws back to a chamber position facing downward (1F).

FIGURE I
Kata Seiunchin

The constant repetition of this basic pattern over a period of years, consisting of literally thousands of repetitions, perfects the basic motor movements associated with the pattern and develops concentration and focus. The kata should be performed in every direction, beginning by facing north, south, east, or west. Eventually, from any given starting position, the student should be able to complete the kata, ending at the original starting position, facing in the starting direction. As a result of this training process, muscle memory develops such that in a real combat situation, the associated response to an attack occurs automatically and without thought.

Intermediate Kata Training

There is a significant difference between learning a kata, and training one-self in kata. Every student is endowed with a level of endurance, strength, and speed that form the primary abilities for performing kata. Endurance is the ability to continue working despite the onset of fatigue and is directly tied to cardio-respiratory performance and correct breathing. Often students may hold their breath while performing a kata leading to fatigue, tension, and sloppy technique; upon completion they may stand gasping for air. Alternatively, due to nervousness or tension, they may breathe too quickly and are thus susceptible to hyperventilation. There are several methods to improve endurance, including repetitions of kata and cross-training with other activities such as running, cycling, or skiing.

Strength is the ability to overcome resistance. It can be improved by weight training with a variety of traditional Okinawan training implements or modern equipment.

Speed is the ability to move quickly. Studies of world-class athletes indicate a higher level of twitch muscles. Thus speed is tied directly to genetic makeup. To increase speed, the student must utilize economy of motion to reduce wasted energy. Therefore, speed is directly tied to improved quality in performing karate techniques, such as in reducing the motion of the shoulder muscle groups during blocks and punches.

Students typically memorize a kata at a given level and then use repetition to improve these primary abilities. However, there are several alternative training methods that can be incorporated into practice to not only improve physical performance but also to achieve harmony between mind and body. These methods systematically isolate and improve a particular aspect of the kata. They allow the student to step back and assess weaknesses in need of additional practice. Each method emphasizes and develops a core set of principals from the Goju-Ryu system.

Hard Principles

Initially, the kata is performed using the hard principals associated with the Sanchin kata (Labbate, 1999). This isolates and develops the principals of structure, movement, and breathing. The kata is performed slowly, with strong tension, and paying close attention to transitioning and positioning. Each blow is supported from the entire shoulder muscle group and locked down at the end of each motion. Movement between stances is accomplished at the same level, without causing the body to bob up and down, or move from side to side. Mental focus allows the weight of the body to be lowered into the stance such that each technique is performed with the body firmly rooted to the ground and supported by correct positioning. In a straddle-leg stance, the legs and feet are positioned at 90 degrees to each other, and the foreleg at 90 degrees to the ground. The back remains straight and supported, the feet move through an arc that bisects the stride. Breathing is coordinated with movement: inhalation occurs between techniques in Seiunchin, and exhalation occurs on each technique. All of these concepts arise directly from the study of Sanchin.

The hard principals are then developed further through exaggeration with weight resistance to enhance both speed and strength. The kata can be performed with traditional training implements such as weighted shoes (*geka*) and dumbbells (*sashi*) as shown in Figure 2A, or straw grips shown in Figure 2B. Modern wrist and ankle weights and weight vests, shown in Figure 2C, can also be used to provide additional resistance. It is important when training with these implements that full power is not put into each technique, this can lead to pulled muscles and strains. Instead, the student reduces power to focus on positioning and strength. When the weights are removed, speed will increase naturally.

FIGURE 2 Resistance Training

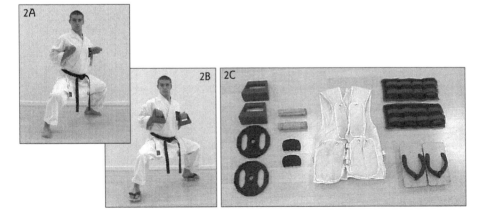

Speed Training

In speed training, the kata is performed as fast and explosively as possible without attention to form or technique. No power or tension is applied in this method, and the techniques are allowed to flow continuously into each as fast as possible. This method deliberately isolates and improves kata performance speed.

Form Training

The goal of form training is to develop perfect technique. The kata is performed slowly with no power or speed. At every movement, stance, position, and form are carefully examined and corrected. Distancing and angles on stances are adjusted, hand techniques are adjusted for correct positioning, and transitions are performed with circular motions. Breathing and movement are carefully coordinated and at the conclusion of each technique the body should be centered and aligned correctly (Labbate, 2000).

Rhythm and Tempo

Every kata has a prescribed cadence or rhythm by virtue of the order of techniques in each fighting sequence. For example, in Seiunchin, the motions from the entry to sumo stance (Fig. 1A) through to the spear hand strike (Fig. 1F) correspond to a single sequence. Each movement in the sequence is performed slowly on a slow count of four, except for the movement in Figure 1E, which is performed on a slow count of two. The complete sequence is repeated three times at the beginning of the kata, first to the right, then to the left, and finally to the right again. There is a slight pause designating the transition between sides and each sequence should be performed symmetrically: a movement on the left, corresponding in length and speed to the same movement on the right. Rhythm training focuses attention on consistency and the balance of timing throughout the kata.

The tempo at which the kata movements are performed is dependent on the student's capabilities. Every student is endowed with a level of strength and speed that improve naturally as training proceeds. Most students exert either too much power or too much speed in their practice. This results in poor form, balance, and symmetry, or over exertion and fatigue. By focusing on tempo, the student learns to harmonize speed and power. The kata is performed as fast a possible, while attempting to maintain form, deliver maximum power in each strike, and correctly lock down the muscle groups at the end of each movement. If the speed is too fast, there is a noticeable sloppiness in form, and as a result strikes lose their power and are ineffective. Conversely, if the kata is performed with too much power, then it will cause jerky and slow motions that will result in fatigue. Tempo training aims to push the boundary of this relationship.

Power Training

Power training is an advanced method based on the "karate drum." In this technique, energy is transferred into techniques from the abdomen (*tanden*) through a subtle shaking motion at the hips (Labbate, 2000; Labbate, 2001). This allows the student to load energy into a technique, transfer it, lock down the technique using Sanchin style structure, and rebound into a countering movement. Figure 3 shows how the movements in Figures 1A, 1B, and 1C are adapted in this method. The guiding principal is that the reverse hand moves first. Notice in Figure 3 how the left hand and hip (reverse in the stance) lead the right. This movement sets up the correct motion to load energy such that subsequent movements rebound into an opponent.

FIGURE 3 Power Training

Focus Training

All of the previous training methods are on the physical level. Unfortunately, a kata performed simply as a sequence of moves is like a book with blank pages. To breathe life into the kata, it is necessary to visualize the fighting movements. Focus training harmonizes speed, power, and technique at normal speed by developing intent. Each movement in a kata is designated a basic level application; for Seiunchin, two such applications are developed later in this paper. The masters of old specifically chose the basic application to allow students to visualize an opponent but protect the kata's more dangerous secrets. In this manner, students were kept at a particular level until their social responsibility and humility were established and they were trusted.

Meditation Training

Meditation isolates and develops the mental aspects to create mind-body harmony and enhance fighting intent. It allows a student to learn about him or herself and assess their strengths and weaknesses. This training method aligns intent with physical training on a subconscious level, so that each movement has a clear purpose.

Meditation can be accomplished in any location or position, for example in the kneeling position (*seiza*) at the training hall (*dojo*) or when simply lying in bed. The student clears the mind and imagines him or herself in an attractive location, perhaps on a beach, at a park, or in the dojo. Then the student mentally performs the entire kata as if watching a video. Any of the intermediate training methods can be adopted during meditation to focus on a specific aspect of kata training. The result of this meditation is that the kata's physical performance is enhanced by the understanding and awareness developed through meditation.

Partner Training

All of the previous training methods focus on independent development and improvement, intended to give a student an understanding of their own level and ability. Partner training is intended to develop an understanding of an opponent: their speed, strength, and ability. It also allows new concepts to be developed such as timing, balancing, and distancing. Generally, sequences from each kata are taken separately and practiced using a variety of positions with the attacker standing in front, behind, or to the side, or with the defender placed at a disadvantage against a wall or on the ground. The intent is for the students to understand the different modes of attack a particular kata sequence is able to deal with, and to be able to recognize a given situation in combat. Having first made contact, it is also valuable for the defender to close their eyes and follow the movements of the attacker through contact, attempting to stick, redirect, and counter their movements (Labbate, 2000; Labbate, 2001).

Partners are joined in friendship and collaboration to help each other improve their skills, timing, and reflexes. It is the instructor's responsibility to ensure that this perspective is transmitted to students. If partner training is allowed to degenerate into a contest, then the value is lost and it becomes simply an issue of winning and ego, rather than an exercise to elevate skill.

Advanced Kata Training

Advanced kata training is focused around the designation of targets and the development of applications to attack them. There are two additional components to the applications: the first involves a variety of joint and wrist locks, arm bars, chokes, and throws; the second involves vital point striking (*kyushojutsu*). The intent is to apply force to carefully chosen points of weakness by understanding the opponent, overcoming their strength or speed, undermining their balance, or smoothly and effectively countering their movements. This is significantly different from blindly performing a given set of movements, in a preset order, toward a general area of the body, such as the head or chest. Like all elements of training, applications have several levels of sophistication. These levels are examined and their medical impact assessed here.

Basic Level Application I

Figure 4 shows how the opening sequence from the Seiunchin kata can be used to counter an opponent that attempts to grab both hands (4A). The counter move is to escape the grab by raising both arms upward in a middle-block fashion (4B). The defender then counterattacks by grabbing the attacker's wrists and (4C) performing a knee strike to the groin (4D).

FIGURE 4
Attacker Attempts to Grab

Medical Implications

The knee strike to the groin will cause immense pain and be debilitating. The attacker will experience any or all of the following: pain, shock, nausea, vomiting, and loss of breath or consciousness. A solid strike can fracture the pubic bone and rupture the bladder. The weakest area is the center of the pubic bone. Once the bone is fractured, the opponent will be rendered in a prone position due to the nauseating pain. Once injured, blood and urine will collect in the abdominal cavity causing tenderness and pain. Typically, the individual will experience an inability to urinate more than a few drops of bloody urine. If untreated, infection may occur. A direct strike can crush the testes and scrotum against the pubic bones resulting in castration.

Basic Level Application 2

An alternative kata application can be used if the attacker attempts to grab at the lapels, as shown in Figure 5A. The attackers' hands are covered and grabbed with the defender's left hand. While the defender's left hand applies a wristlock on the opponent's left hand, the defender's right performs a palm-heel strike into the attacker's groin (5B); this corresponds to Figure 1d in the kata. While the defender's left hand continues to maintain a wristlock on the opponent, the defender's right hand grabs the attacker's lapel (5C); this corresponds to Figure 1E. Finally, the defender pulls into a chamber position while applying a left knife-hand strike (*shuto*) to the ear (5D); this corresponds to Figure 1F.

FIGURE 5
Attacker Attempts to Push

Medical Implications

As explained earlier, a severe blow to the testicles will cause the attacker to experience any or all of pain, shock, nausea, vomiting, and loss of breath or consciousness. The attack in Figure 5D directly strikes the ear. A percussive type shock to the eardrum (tympanac membrane) expands the auditory canal and eustachian tube with compressed air. The impact by such a blow will cause the small blood vessels and capillaries of the outer ear to rupture, thus swelling the ear. Because the air expands in volume as it travels through the narrow eustachian tube, the capillaries inside the canal, and even the eardrum, can rupture and swell. This will cause the eustachian tube to swell completely shut. The sensory nerves inside the auditory canal and eardrum contribute to hearing and balance. The locked air pressure inside produces severe pain, dizziness, and even unconsciousness. Permanent hearing loss can result.

Intermediate Application

Figure 6 shows an intermediate application in which the attacker grabs the defender with a bear hug from behind (6A). The defender grabs the attacker's fingers by moving both hands upwards (6B); this corresponds to Figure 1B. The defender then counters by grabbing the attacker's fingers in a downward fashion (6C); this corresponds to Figure 1C. While maintaining a finger lock on the opponent with the left hand, the defender takes a right step forward and moves back around to the left (approximately 270 degrees). The defender then pops the back of the elbow and grabs the triceps with the right hand (6d); this corresponds to Figure 1D. Finally, while maintaining a finger lock with the left hand, the defender shifts the right hand toward the back of the opponent's elbow and steps toward the left; the right hand then moves up and inward, while the left hand snaps in an outward fashion thus dislocating the elbow and fingers (6E); this corresponds to Figures 1E and 1F.

FIGURE 6
Elbow Application

Medical Implications

Figure 7 shows a schematic of the elbow manipulated in the latter parts of this application. A strike to the superficial branch located on the forearm, approximately three inches down from the top of the elbow will cause the arm and hand to suffer a dull aching pain. Since the radial nerve is affected, the opponent will have difficulty making a fist because the muscle is weakened. Popping the elbow joint located at the back of a straightened arm can dislocate the elbow (ulna from humerus) and break the arm. If the blow is strong enough, it will affect the ulnar nerve in approximately 25 percent of cases (Haymaker, 1953: 133–184). The ulnar nerve runs distally (away from the point of origin) and crosses the elbow joint to the forearm. The affected area, commonly referred as the "funny bone," will cause the opponent to experience a pinprick-like shock down the forearm and hand.

If a supracondylar fracture at the humerus' distal end shown in Figure 7 occurs the opponent will experience diffuse swelling in the elbow region and intense pain, thus disabling the arm. The bicep and tricep muscles can be torn if the resultant trauma is severe. The radial nerve is most commonly injured from fractures (Haymaker, 1953). The individual may experience nerve compression or bone fragments can even sever the nerve. Pain, loss of sensation, and possible paralysis of parts of the arm and/or hand may result with this type of injury. If the brachial artery is pinched or severed, tissue damage will occur and may develop into gangrene in extreme cases.

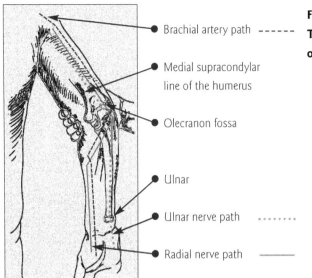

Brachial artery path ------

Medial supracondylar
line of the humerus

Olecranon fossa

Ulnar

Ulnar nerve path ·········

Radial nerve path ———

FIGURE 7
The Structure
of the Elbow

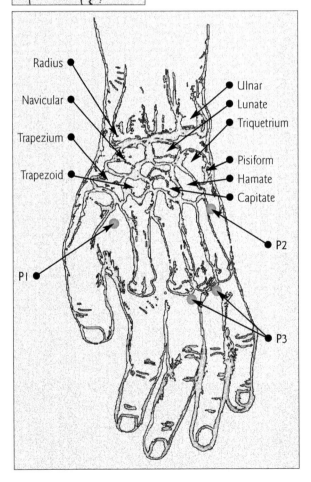

Radius

Navicular

Trapezium

Trapezoid

PI

Ulnar

Lunate

Triquetrium

Pisiform

Hamate

Capitate

P2

P3

FIGURE 8:
Hand and Wrist

Figure 8 shows
the structure of the
human wrist and hand
manipulated through a
wristlock or finger-hold
in this application.

The fingers are particularly vulnerable to being sprained or broken, which can make it difficult for the opponent to make a fist. The radial artery, flexor tendons, and medial nerves are reachable in the inner side of the wrist. If the defender digs their fingers or knuckles centrally in this area at the median nerve, it will produce a sharp pain in the forearm and a weakened feeling in the hand. Grabbing the back of the hand can produce severe pain in the opponent's hand and arm. The key pressure points depicted in Figure 8 are: between the thumb and the index finger (P1), where the radial nerve is exposed against the side of the second metacarpal bone; along the little finger side of the fourth metacarpal (P2), where the ulnar nerve is exposed; and between the knuckles of the middle and ring fingers (P3). Finger holds in any of these areas can be used to control the opponent's movement and weaken the grip. The wrist is composed of eight carpal bones in two rows. The navicular (scaphoid bone) is the most commonly fractured bone and is located on the radial side of the carpus (above the radius near your thumb). The lunate located proximal to the capitate (above the radius near the middle finger) is the second most commonly fractured bone. The triquetrium is located distal (opposite) to the ulnar styloid process (above the ulnar near the pinkie finger) and is also vulnerable to injury and the third most commonly fractured bone (Hoppenfeld, 1976: 65-71). Once the wrist is fractured, the hand is useless.

Advanced Level Application

Figure 9 shows an advanced application in which the attacker grabs at the chest (9A). The defender moves both hands simultaneously upward and traps both forearms (9B); this corresponds to the beginning of the movement in Figure 1b. The defender then applies a right and left knife-hand strike to the neck (9C); corresponding to the conclusion of the movement in Figure 1C. The defender then thumb rakes the eyes downward (9D–E); corresponding to Figure 1C. While the attacker tries to maintain a hold on the defenders lapel, the opponent's left hand is trapped and a right knife-hand strike to the side or back of the head is performed (9F); corresponding to Figure 1d. The back of the attacker's neck is grabbed with the right hand, while striking the chin with the left hand (9G). A quick pull with the right hand and a push with the left hand snaps the attacker's neck (9G). This corresponds to Figures 1E and 1F.

FIGURE 9
Application Resulting
in Severe Injury

Medical Implications

The thumb rake to the eyes can cause hemorrhage and loss of sight. Disruption of the cornea, lens, and rectus muscle results. The eyelid may be vulnerable to a tear by the striking fingers, thereby increasing the risk for infection. If the strike is severe, the optic nerve may be injured. Jennett et al. (in Bailes et al, 1989: 137–156) reported this was the most common cranial nerve injury seen in head injuries. Retinal detachment occurred in 7 percent of martial arts related injuries (Rabadi, Birrer, Jordan, 2000: 297–303). In both scenarios, emergent surgical intervention is required as treatment.

FIGURE 10-A

Muscles of the Neck

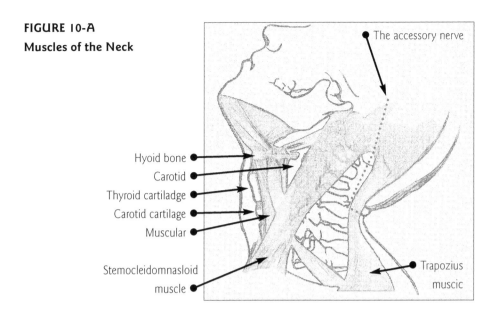

Figure 10-A shows a schematic of the head and neck manipulated in Figures 9F and 9. Neck and head injuries are the result of three distinct types of stresses generated by a force applied to the head (Cantu, 2000: 137–156). The first two are compressive and tensile or linear forces. An example would be an athlete who is standing still and struck by a moving object. Focal injuries are produced such as brain contusions or intracranial hematoma. The third force is a rotational or shearing force. This creates diffuse brain injuries from a concussion to coma. These injuries can result in other deficits such as cognition, memory, attention, language, and psychosocial adaptation and even death. The most common acute traumatic brain injury in martial arts is cerebral concussion (Rabadi, Birrer, & Jordan, 2000: 297–303). This injury can become cumulative. The chronic traumatic brain injury results in Parkinsonism or progressive difficulty in ambulation, coordination, and display of cognitive dysfunction (Jordan, 2000: 339–346).

The sternocleidomastoid muscle and trapezius shown in Figure 10-A share a continuous attachment along the base of the skull to the mastoid process where they split and have a different attachment along the clavicle. They share the accessory nerve (cranial nerve XI). A strike approximately an inch below the angle of the jaw will bruise both the sternocleidomastoid muscle and accessory nerve. This causes pain and partial temporary paralysis of the neck and shoulder area. The carotid artery and jugular vein shown in Figure 10-B runs along the carotid tubercle of C6. A blow in this region can cause occlusion, dissection or even a thrombic emboli into the intracranial vessels and resultant stroke (Rabadi, Birrer, & Jordan 2000: 297–303) and (McCrory, 2000: 200–209). There is a documented case where a 26-year old sustained a carotid dissection and resultant hemispheric infarction after sustaining a knife-hand strike to the carotid artery (Fig. 10-B). There are also documented cases with vertebral artery dissection. A strike to the vagus nerve produces an inhibitory effect, slowing the heart rate and lowering the blood pressure. A severe strike in this region can produce loss of consciousness (Gott, 1997: 110–113) and a deep contusion.

FIGURE 10-B: Arteries of the Neck

The dote represents the accessory & vagus nerve which originates from the medulla oblongata (base of the stem)

Internal cartoid artery

C3

Vertebral artery

Hyoid bone
External carotid artery
Thyroid cartilage
Cricoid cartilage
Common carotid artery
Trachea
Jugular vein's path

A dislocation to the thyroid cartilage or the tracheal ring (Fig. 10-B) can occur by snapping the neck. Suffocation typically results due to the windpipe swelling shut. A severe blow to the back of the neck or disruption to the C3 vertebrae results in spinal cord injury. The individual may need to be ventilated since respiratory dysfunction occurs (Bailes, Cerullo, & Engelhard, 1989: 137–156). Cervical spine injuries can be as simple as soft tissue injuries (whiplash) to actual fractures or dislocation of the cervical spine. Although rare, neurologic injuries can be very debilitating and can cause death. Extreme awareness and education is needed to fully understand the medical implications. Medical authorities advise that preventive guidelines need to be followed to make the martial arts safer (Rabadi, Birrer, & Jordan, 2000: 297–303). As noted in "Article 3: Advice on Correct Etiquette" in the *Bubishi*:

Regardless of whether people study quanfa for health, recreation, or self-defense, everyone must understand that it is not to be misused. Therefore, teachers should have their disciples swear an oath. In this oath disciples must pledge to never intentionally hurt anyone or do anything unjust.

– McCarthy, 1995: 68

Conclusion

This chapter has described a variety of principals that can be employed in kata training to elevate skill level and improve self-awareness and focus. The techniques allow a student to understand their strengths and weaknesses and to focus on areas where improvement is needed. At the most basic levels, these techniques gradually breathe life into a kata and aid the student. At the advanced levels, this chapter has shown that there are dangerous consequences.

Over the last few decades, techniques that were formerly passed down by oral tradition, from father to son or a cherished student, have been published openly for commercial gain. For example, the *Bubishi*, once a carefully guarded secret text, is now widely available through a variety of publishers. Details of vital point striking have appeared in numerous books. Thus the controls that the masters once exerted, carefully picking worthy students, with impeccable character and social responsibility, to carry forward the art have now been compromised. In recent years, this process has degenerated into shameful demonstrations and seminars where students have been struck, and in some cases made unconscious, to illustrate the ideas. An attack on an unwitting student requires no skill, and serves no purpose other than to inflate the instructor's ego. These actions set the wrong example entirely: there is no honor, integrity, respect, or courtesy that can be learned from such irresponsible behavior. This chapter has shown that there are serious, unpredictable medical risks associated with vital point striking. The real challenge to an instructor is not to demonstrate the effects, but rather to advance students through the levels of teaching at a pace that is consistent with responsible behavior and student safety.

Bibliography

Bailes, J., Cerullo, L., & Engelhard, H. (1989). Neurologic assessment and management of head injuries. In Paul Meyer, Jr. (Ed.), *Surgery of spine trauma* (pp. 137–156). New York: Churchill Living Stone, Inc.

Cantu, M. (Ed.) (2000). *Biomechanics of head injury in neurologic athletic head and spine injuries*. Philadelphia: W. B. Saunders Co.

Gott, V. (1997). The heart. In George Zuidema (Ed.), *The John Hopkins atlas of human functional anatomy* (pp. 110–113). Baltimore: John Hopkins University Press.

Haymaker, W., & Woodhall, B. (1953). *Peripheral nerve injuries: Principles of diagnosis*, 2nd edition. Philadelphia: W. B. Saunders Co.

Hoppenfield, S. (1976). *Physical examination of the spine and extremities*. New York: Appleton-Century-Crofts.

Jordan, B. (2000). Head and spine injuries in boxing, (pp. 297–303). In Robert Cantu (Ed.), *Biomechanics of head injury in neurologic athletic head and spine injuries*. Philadelphia: W. B. Saunders Co.

Labbate, M. (1999). Elements of advanced karate techniques. *Journal of Asian Martial Arts*, 8(2), 80–95.

Labbate, M. (2000). Developing advanced Goju-Ryu techniques: Illustrated in the rising block. *Journal of Asian Martial Arts*, 9(1), 56–69.

Labbate, M. (2001). Tensho kata: Goju-Ryu's secret treasure. *Journal of Asian Martial Arts*, 10(1), 84–99.

McCarthy, P. (1995). *The bible of karate: Bubishi*. Rutland, VT: Charles E. Tuttle.

McCrory, P. (2000). Strokes in athletes, (pp. 200–209). In Robert Cantu (Ed.), *Biomechanics of head injury in neurologic athletic head and spine injuries*. Philadelphia: W. B. Saunders Co.

Rabadi, M., Birrer R., & Jordan, B. (2000). Head and spine injuries (pp. 297–303). In Robert Cantu, (Ed.), *Biomechanics of head injury in neurologic athletic head and spine injuries*. Philadelphia: W. B. Saunders Co.

Acknowledgments

The author would like to thank Ken Yonemura, M.D., and Grace Noda, medical consultant, for their aid in describing the medical implications of the karate principals in this paper. The author would like to thank Marc Gervais and Michael Egnato for performing the kata movements and applications for this paper.

The Lost Secrets of Okinawan Goju-Ryu: What the Kata Shows

by Giles Hopkins, M.A.

The author training with the oar
(*eku*) at Matayoshi Shinpo's dojo.
All photos courtesy of G. Hopkins.

Introduction

On a hot July evening in 1986, I was standing in the martial arts training hall listening to Matayoshi Shinpo explain one of the postures of kata Kakuho, a Kingai-Ryu system form (*kata*). We had been walking up and down the floor in crane stance, toes of one foot curled under ready to throw small pebbles or sand into attacker's face, arms out to the side like wings. Matayoshi had come down earlier to watch *kobudo* (ancient weapons art) training. When we had finished, we began training some of the empty-hand katas of Matayoshi's family system and our own Goju-Ryu. It was already late in the evening. Sometimes Matayoshi would stop and try to explain something with the few English words he knew and then laugh.

Left to right: Kimo Wall, the author, Paul Gorter,
and Matayoshi Shinpo at Higa Seko's grave site.

"You no show," he would say. "Okay?" That summer, sitting in an ice cream
shop in downtown Naha, Matayoshi had heard a particularly blaring American
pop song. The singers' voices were harsh and nasal as they repeated the chorus,
"Show me, show me." Matayoshi had asked what the words meant, and from then
on, he used the words frequently, and laugh.

At the moment, however, he was trying to explain how one of the moves
in the kata was used. Though the application was obvious, we couldn't figure out
what he was trying to get across. With Matayoshi's peculiar collection of a couple
dozen English words or phrases and our handful of Japanese words, it was like some
hilarious game of charades. Matayoshi would bend down and pretend to pull up
clumps of imaginary grass (we later realized). Then he would rear back with both
arms up in front of his body, elbows in, forearms vertical, wrists bent so that the
hands, held above the head, formed claws. Then he would stop and hold one hand
up with index finger and thumb spread apart.

"You know?" he would ask. Of course we didn't.

Finally, someone went for a small pocket dictionary.

"*Mushi*," Matayoshi said, pointing to the word, "Insect."

"*Midori.*"

We all laughed. Matayoshi had only been trying to explain that it was a praying mantis technique. Nothing more. It made me wonder how many other things we had missed in translation that summer, and how situations not so different from this one may have affected the Okinawan martial arts in general and Goju-Ryu specifically. Were secrets lost in translation? What sorts of things had other students misunderstood along the way?

Interpreting the Meaning of Katas

The history of Goju-Ryu has been researched, second and third generation teachers have been interviewed, and, most importantly perhaps, the katas themselves have been scrutinized and analyzed. Each new journal article seems to have another theory about katas. Every teacher seems to have a new and different explanation of kata applications (*bunkai*). Internet discussion groups abound with imaginative discoveries of kata's meaning.

However, all of this discussion raises a far more perplexing question: How could so many practitioners be at odds about the meaning of things so fundamental to their art, to what they practice on a daily basis? Why do so many of these articles and books seem to be archeological treasure hunts in search of the Rosetta Stone—in search of something to unlock the key to Goju-Ryu as a system? In other words, why don't we know what kata movements really mean? Why are we still debating applications, looking for what the original intent of the various Goju-Ryu katas must have been?

Seated, left to right: the author, Matayoshi Shinpo, and Kina Seiko. Standing: Oshiro Zenei and Miyazato (Matayoshi's brother-in-law).

Matayoshi Shinpo demonstrating Kakuho
kata from his family system, Kingai-Ryu.

As it stands now, the kata applications mean whatever a "legitimate" instructor says they mean. And there is considerable disagreement. Every school seems to have its claim, well-established through various lineages, to authenticity. In the spirit of equanimity and brotherhood, students and teachers alike will argue that there are an almost infinite number of applications. So, if there is not one "right" application for each move, there would seem at least to be no wrong answers. Or, to rectify the disparity, some suggest that there are multiple levels of understanding. But these are not answers; they're rationalizations and only serve to confuse the issue. In the *Journal of Asian Martial Arts*, a Goju-Ryu practitioner forwarded the theory that Shisochin was an answer to Sanseiru: that if you superimpose one kata over the other, the techniques of one seem to show counters to the other (Toth, 2001).

Though the origins of katas are certainly lost in a distant past—as are the legendary creators of these katas—I find it hard to imagine that whoever made and formalized kata movements could have been so intentionally cryptic. It is as if the katas themselves were some elaborate Rorschach test, where different people see different things. At the very least, this kind of analysis serves to illustrate the dilemma.

Without becoming too philosophical, it isn't difficult to see how this can happen. It is easy to assign meaning, to rationalize an interpretation however idiosyncratic. After all, man is the great signifier. We can and do find meaning in the seeming randomness of nature, the chaos of the universe, the rantings of madmen, or the brush strokes of an elephant with a paintbrush. Why not kata?

The sad thing is that given this state of confusion with katas, some have, lamentably though I suppose understandably, "thrown out the baby with the bath water" and chosen to point an accusatory finger and shout, "the emperor has no clothes!" as Nathan Johnson does in *Barefoot Zen* (2000: 125). That is to say, long time practitioners will throw their hands up in frustration—and Johnson is certainly not alone here—exclaiming that the katas don't mean anything, the movements are just movements and there is no system to be understood. As Johnson puts it: "People looking for a systematic or progressive development of attack and defense techniques in the traditional forms will be disappointed" (2000: 122). It's an understandable frustration—a radical belief born out of confusion—but also mistaken.

Katas in Historical Perspective

I would suggest that the reason there is such debate about katas and their applications may lie in the turbulent nature of the 20th century or, in Goju-Ryu's case, in Miyagi Chojun's untimely death at the age of 65. But in reality, I think it may have more to do with the very nature of karate training today and how it developed over the past 100 years.

Consider the direction that karate had taken in Okinawa in the early 20th century. Karate had already become a part of the Okinawan school system as early as 1909 (Toguchi, 1976: 13–14; McCarthy, 1999: 48). Whatever the reasons for this move, it would have far-reaching consequences. A martial art practiced by schoolchildren is necessarily very different from the system of self-defense trained by the Okinawan warrior class (*bushikaikyuu*) or the monk-warriors of China who may have developed the original katas.

With Gekisai I and Gekisai II—and various other "training" subjects added later by other teachers—Miyagi Chojun created "generic" katas that could more safely be taught to young people, to students. A beginner's curriculum based on these training subjects would be less lethal and a teacher would not be giving away the art's "secrets." But one would also not be studying the essence of Goju-Ryu. This is apparent from the opening move of Gekisai I. The upper-level block as it is done in this kata is not found anywhere in Goju-Ryu's "classical" katas. The Gekisai katas and basic training (*kihon*) may have served to popularize karate and improve its image—one of the goals that Miyagi seems to suggest in his 1934 *Outline of Karate-do* (McCarthy, 1999)—changing the public perception of the martial arts from the pugilistic occupation of warriors and street toughs to a systematized activity of physical conditioning. But a dojo curriculum based on these exercises would only serve to mask the real techniques, the essence, of the classical katas.

This seems to have been a goal that many Okinawan karate masters shared: not intentionally to hide real karate, but to popularize a version that would be more acceptable to the public. Katas were preserved but applications received less emphasis. Group exercise and physical conditioning replaced traditional application of technique because teachers like Itosu Ankoh considered the techniques "too dangerous" for schoolchildren. As McCarthy notes, "the emphasis shifted from a self-defense art to a cultural recreation for physical fitness" (1999: 106). This shift in emphasis was further solidified in a 1936 meeting of Okinawan karate masters. Although Miyagi clearly states that "the classical kata must remain," there is a not-so-subtle push from some quarters to standardize technique and separate it from its Chinese roots. In line with his earlier interests in changing the public's perception of karate, Miyagi even suggests that "suitable kata, with both offensive and defensive [sic], for students from elementary school to university level should be developed" (McCarthy, 1999: 65).

This shift in emphasis continued in the post-World War II years. Dan Smith, a long-time Shorin-Ryu teacher, argues that the spread of karate to mainland Japan led to teachers who "did not stay with the Okinawans long enough to learn and the karate that was taught in the beginning was kihon [fundamentals]."

The same thing affected karate in Okinawa after the war, Smith goes on to say, for a variety of reasons. The older teachers in Okinawa—those that knew the "secrets"—far from any intentional effort at hiding technique, Smith writes, were merely responding to "the changing times." Smith suggests that they "designed their instruction to meet the perceived needs of the day....[E]mphasis was put on kihon, kata and *jiu kumite* [free sparring]" (Smith, Letter 1).

Others have not been so charitable. Anthony Marquez, writing in the now defunct *Bugeisha* magazine, argues that even second generation Okinawan teachers didn't know the old applications. Marquez writes that Masanobu Shinjo told him that the "old techniques died with the past generations" (Marquez, 1996: 13). So, for whatever reason, Okinawan karate underwent a significant change in the 20th century, whether this was due to an effort to popularize karate or because many younger teachers were ill equipped to teach the classical curriculum or that the older teachers didn't really know or were merely being accommodating.

In any case, this is the karate that we see practiced today—both here and in most Okinawan dojos. It is not real Goju-Ryu. It is schoolboy karate. Certainly it can be effective, both for self-defense and physical conditioning, but it is not the same karate that we find in the classical Goju-Ryu katas. It is also important to remember that the lessons of one do not necessarily translate into an understanding of the other.

Matayoshi Shinpo
visiting the author's dojo.

As evidenced from early demonstrations, Miyagi Chojun's karate consisted of "throwing and grappling techniques." According to Higaonna Morio's research, Miyagi was renown for his "pulling down techniques...*sabaki* (body movement)... and *muchimi* (sticky hands)" (Higaonna, 1985: 28–29). This gives us some clue as to the real nature of Goju-Ryu and techniques found within the classical katas.

Sadly, the training tools, like the Gekisai katas, shed little if any light on the meaning of classical katas and their self-defense applications. In fact, the training subjects and the two-person sets developed by Toguchi Seikichi and others work contrary to many of the principles found in the classical katas. And it is for this reason, I believe, that the real meaning of the Goju-Ryu katas has remained a mystery to so many people for so long.

Seeing Katas for What They Are

However, the mystery can be unraveled by the katas themselves. Everything the traditional karate practitioner needs to know about Goju-Ryu as a system is contained in the classical katas: Saifa, Seiunchin, Shisochin, Sepai, Sanseiru, Sesan, Kururunfa, and Suparimpei.

The only thing one needs to do in analyzing the katas—in studying applications correctly—is to apply martial principles to the movements, and this is exactly what has not been done. We have looked at katas as if they were arbitrary collections of techniques—so many contained in each kata, we are told, that it would take a lifetime to master just one—ignoring the lessons contained in the patterns themselves. Or, we have attempted to explain the movement as an imaginary battle against multiple attackers. Both of these explanations—while seemingly plausible—are at the very least misleading. Again, one need only apply the principles to see the katas as they were originally meant to be seen. If we don't, we are left with a generic art of punching and kicking—not much better than schoolboy karate. As the Chinese classics put it: "If we do not practice according to the applications of the principles, we can work forever without developing a superior art" (Wile, 1983: 71).

The principles are basically simple. Always move off the centerline whenever possible. As the Chinese classics state: "We must quickly evade by withdrawing our center and attacking from the side" (Wile, 1983: 67). Smith states this a bit more colloquially when he says, "Get out of the way" (Smith, Letter 3). This is the first principle. If the various katas were not meant to demonstrate this principle, then all of the katas would be done in a straight line. But they are not. The steps and turns—indeed, most of the direction changes within a kata—show where the attack is coming from, and, consequently, how to get out of the way of the attack or how to step off the centerline.

Repeatedly, what one will notice in practicing kata is that one turns to step off the centerline that the attacker is advancing along. If one applies this principle to the first move of the Sepai kata (see illustration, 1A & 1E), one can see that contrary to what is commonly taught—that the attack is a frontal attack and one is merely stepping back along the line of attack—the attack is really from the west. The step back into a horse stance side-steps the attack and removes one's center, placing the defender in a 90 degree relationship to the attacker.

The first movement in Goju-Ryu is often to side-step the opponent, whether this is to the outside (usually) or the inside. But so often, dojo training seems to emphasize Goju-Ryu's hardness. We train doing the Sanchin kata or arm-toughening drills (*koteikitai*) with the idea that we will stand squarely in front of an attacker and be able to take whatever he doles out.

However, what katas more often show is that Goju-Ryu is initially soft, using angles and stepping to avoid the attack, blocking and hooking in circular motions, tying the attacker up, using his own momentum against him, redirecting the attack. As the Chinese classics remind us, we should "meet hardness with softness" (Wile, 1983: 91). Goju-Ryu is first soft, then hard.

Another principle one should keep in mind is, in a sense, more historical. Karate, and martial arts in general, was not originally intended as a sport or a casual pursuit restricted to the dojo or community center. It was a deadly martial art meant to be used in combat, intended to protect or save one's life. It was not intended for competition, a later modification or 20th century innovation when "the Butokukai required that there be a measurement of skill of the new martial art, 'karate'.... With this innovation karate introduced a new scenario ... mutually agreed upon combat" (Smith, Letter 6). In traditional karate, the important point is that the attacker was fully committed to his attack, and this should be remembered when one looks at any application.

By the same token, the defender was fully committed to preserving his or her own life. The techniques were not intended to give the attacker a second chance. They were meant to be used only as a last resort. If we keep this idea in mind when looking at katas, we tend to see a different level of brutality for lack of a more euphemistic term—techniques that don't merely fight the arms of the attacker but go straight to more vital body parts. The classical katas teach one to block the arms, but attack the head. If we begin to look at katas in this way, the katas become much more lethal, and, I believe, more historical, truer to the original intent of the katas and their applications. At the same time, all of the techniques will begin to fit together and the combinations of moves will begin to make sense.

To illustrate, I will try to show how the techniques of the Sepai kata demonstrate these principles. The applications adhere to the kata's movement, but the rhythm at which the techniques are executed may vary considerably from what one usually practices in solo kata. What should become immediately apparent is that the kata is a collection of sequences or techniques done in combination against one attacker, not multiple opponents. Stepping and directional changes generally show where the attack is coming from and provide the defender with a graphic illustration of how to step off the centerline or how one should block and enter. Each sequence begins with a block and entry technique, and ends with the opponent on the ground. This is what is meant by the Okinawan saying, "*karate ni sente nashi*" ("in karate there is no first attack"). However, it is not just the kata that demonstrates this idea, but each sequence within the kata.

TECHNICAL SECTION

Sepai Kata *(Sepai = eighteen)*

First Sequence:

Facing north, the kata begins with two circular arm movements, stepping back with the left foot into a horse stance with feet at 45-degree angles (*shiko dachi*) (1A). Take two steps forward in the basic stance, followed by a series of palm-to-palm grasping techniques (1B & C). Drop into a horse stance as the right elbow and forearm is brought up (1D).

Application:

The attacker is coming from the west, stepping in with a right punch. By stepping back with the left foot into a horse stance, the kata is showing lateral movement, stepping off the centerline. The defender is sidestepping the attack and blocking with the left open hand. The right arm is brought over the attacking arm behind the opponent's head, coming down on the back of the neck (1E). Stepping up with the left foot, the left hand is brought underneath to the opponent's chin, the right hand is on top of the head (1F). Bring the opponent's head around with the right hand and secure with both hands, advancing with the right foot (1G). Step in behind and drop into a right-foot forward horse stance with a neck break (1H).

Second Sequence:

The next series of techniques, done from a back stance (*kokutso dachi*), begins with what appears to be a left open-hand downward strike, while the right open-hand and forearm is held at chest level, palm down (2A). This is followed by a hooking block and a *shuto* (knife-edge attack) in a front stance (2B). The next technique is a front kick (2C) and grabbing technique, returning to a horse stance (2D), followed by a downward elbow or forearm strike (2E).

Application:

Step in to the north with a sweeping left open-hand block in a clock-wise direction. The attacker is stepping in with a right punch that is blocked by the left sweeping block (2F), carrying the attack down in a clockwise direction and then, sticking to the attacking arm, carrying it up to the left in a trapping block. Pivoting to a left-foot forward front stance, the left hand opens the target as it is brought up. At the same time, a right knife-hand (*shuto*) attacks the opponent's head or neck (2G). The arms should move in unison here. The knee and foot are then brought up into the attacker's stomach and groin (2H). Stepping back into a horse stance, the attacker is pulled down with both hands (2I) and a downward elbow attack is used to finish him off (2J). It should be noted that the hands begin in the open-hand position to attack and then close to indicate a grab or grasping of the opponent.

Third Sequence:

The next series of moves begins in a front stance (*zenkutsu dachi*) and pulls back into a cat stance (*neko ashi dachi*), while executing what appears to be middle-level block. The left open-hand sweeps across the body, closing into a fist, and comes to rest beneath the right elbow (3A). The right arm, with closed fist, sweeps across the body, ending in lower-level position (3B). The right arm is then brought up into a middle-level blocking position as the weight shifts back into a cat stance. The right hand then opens (3C). The next move is a step and turn to the original front into a basic stance while the left arm is brought up and over the right, both arms finishing in front of the chest with closed fists (3D). The next technique—an upper-level circular arm movement and a lower-level open-hand attack—is executed with a turning step to the rear into a basic stance. The left arm circles counterclockwise to the ribs while the right hand follows the right foot, attacking with the palm, fingers down, palm forward, at thigh level (3E).

Application:

Turning to the south into a right-foot-forward front stance, block the attacker's punch with the left open hand, while hooking and grabbing the arm. The attacker is stepping in to attack from the east with a right punch. The right arm is brought around the attacker's head, bringing the attacker's head down into the right knee of the front stance (3F–G). As the attacker is "released," the defender shifts back into a cat stance, pulling the opponent back by grabbing the head or hair with the right open hand, while maintaining control of the opponent's punching arm (3H). The right knee may be employed here as the shift into a cat stance indicates. Then, stepping in behind the attacker, the left arm is brought around the opponent's neck and thrust up in an attack to the throat (3I). The left hand then opens, to control the attacker's chin, and, turning to the left, the opponent is thrown to the rear. The right hand continues in a lower-level attack to facilitate the throw (3J).

Fourth Sequence:

The next series of movements is repeated to both the left and right sides, using an advancing natural stance (*renoji dachi*) (4A), followed by a step into a horse stance (4B), a throw, and a double attack, dropping into a low horse stance (4C).

Application:

Step in to the southeast corner with the left foot while executing a circular sweeping left open-hand block in a clockwise direction (4D). The opponent is attacking with a right punch, from the southeast. As the sweeping block opens the target, the right open hand attacks the opponent's face. Continue the attack as the right foot steps in behind the attacker's right leg and hip (4E). Bring the right knee up and throw. Finish with a double punch or using both hands to drive the opponent into the ground (4F).

Fifth Sequence:

Step back into a horse stance, executing a lower-level block (5A).

Application:

The attacker is coming from the east, attacking with a right punch. Looking to the east, step back into a horse stance to block and grab with the right hand, as the left forearm is brought down on the attacker's neck and head (5B–C). Here the fourth sequence is repeated to the southwest corner, reversing the sides. This is followed by a repetition of the fifth sequence to the west, reversing the sides.

Sixth Sequence:

The next technique involves a step into a cat stance with a middle-level block and upper-level hooking punch (6A). This is followed by a pivoting of the body wherein the weight is transferred to the other foot and the hands are brought down to the side (6B). This is followed by a jump or step to the front, landing in a cross-legged stance with the left foot behind the right, and the hands in reverse position to the previous middle-level and upper-level block and attack (6C). This is followed by a counter-clockwise pivot to end facing the east (6D).

Application:

With a left-hand attack coming from the east, step off the centerline to the south with the right foot. In a left foot forward cat stance, block the opponent's attack with the left arm and attack to the head with the right (6E). The right arm is then brought down onto the attacker's left arm (6F) and hooks the arm as the "jump" is executed. The right foot then steps in to the north, behind the attacker. The left punch then attacks to the opponent's head as the left foot is brought in behind the right foot (6G). Then, pivoting sharply to the left, as the feet unwind, in a counter-clockwise three-quarter turn, the attacker is thrown to the east (6H), the original direction of the opponent's attack. This entire sequence should be done in a single flowing motion without stops. It will be noted that this throwing sequence is the reverse of the sequence that ends the kata.

Seventh Sequence:

This sequence is repeated on both the right and left sides after pivoting from the cross-legged stance into an open-hand block in a basic stance (7A). After again pivoting the body, execute a downward motion or strike with the left arm (7B), followed by backfist (*uraken*) or a forearm attack (7C). Again, the stance pivots, while executing a middle-level block (7D). The next move involves an open-hand grabbing block, front instep kick (7E), and undercut attack (7F), ending in a horse stance.

Application:

The final position of the previous throw and the initial technique of this next sequence almost overlap. Block the opponent's left punch with the right palm. The left hand simultaneously attacks to the opponent's head or neck (7G). Pivot in place, using the left arm to bring the opponent's head down in a clock-wise direction (7H). Attack to the back of the neck with the left forearm (7I). Pivot back toward the east and use the right forearm to come under the opponent's neck or to attack and control the other side of the neck and head (7J). The right hand then grabs the opponent, as the right knee lifts to strike the groin or midsection or as an instep kick (7K), and then the left undercut is used to attack (7L).

The seventh sequence is repeated to the left side or west.

Eighth Sequence:

The final series of techniques begins with a step and turn into a curious stance that has the heel of the right foot in contact with the left toes at roughly a 90-degree angle. The hands are brought into the body, palms facing each other, one above and one below the solar plexus (8A). Retreating into a cat stance, a throw is executed with the hands rotating in a clockwise direction (8B), followed by a hammer-fist strike (8C).

Application:

With a right hand attack coming from the west, step off the centerline to the south with the left foot, while blocking the right punch with a left open-hand block (8D). The left-hand block comes to rest, palm up, on the top of the attacking arm. Stepping up into a cross-footed stance, right foot in front of left, the right hand, forearm, and elbow are brought across the attacker's face (8E). Now facing north, step back into a left-foot-forward cat stance, as the attacker's head is brought down and the left arm is brought up in a clockwise direction (8F). This series is completed as the left hand grabs the attacker's head and the right hammerfist attacks (8G). As in many other katas, the final position is in a cat stance to show that the front knee may be used to attack. This completes the kata.

Conclusion

It has taken me many years to get to a point where I can see katas in this way. This was not an instant realization. However, what should be immediately apparent to any Goju-Ryu practitioner is that the applications are different when one applies these principles to a study of katas. The paradigm that has informed—or misinformed—the study of kata applications in the past, taken from basic dojo drills or the Butokukai construct of mutually agreed upon combat for contest or testing purposes, actually affects how one looks at the techniques of kata even when applied to the classical subjects. One cannot study the applications of classical katas as if one is standing squarely in front of the opponent, feet planted, doing basic drills. One must take into account the katas' patterns and what they are attempting to show us. In other words, the applications of the hand techniques must also employ side-stepping and angular movement. Once this is done, and the blocking and entry techniques have been found, then the katas will be seen as collections of combinations. It will also reinforce the notion that the katas' original intent was to show specific martial principles and applications, not a multitude of possible interpretations.

I have used the Sepai kata to illustrate just a few of these principles. The same lessons, of course, can be applied to any of the classical forms. And certainly there are other principles that are also helpful. But there are some caveats as well. Great care should be taken to let go of preconceived notions of what Goju-Ryu is and what it is not. As I have so often heard from my teacher, one should always train with an "open mind." However, one of the difficulties is that the formalities of training, or what we are used to, get in the way. The execution of the kata moves—particularly when it is performed within the dojo alongside others—sets up a rhythm that is at once metronomic and robotic. For teaching purposes, we regulate the speed within the kata and establish stopping points. All of this is artificial and, in fact, arbitrary to some extent.

Kata is dynamic. If the techniques are done against an attacker, they will flow in a continuous and uninterrupted stream. As the Chinese classics suggest, movements should be "continuous, circular and unending. Continuity without interruption" (Wile, 1983: 13). This is the manner in which the various sequences in the Goju-Ryu katas are meant to be done. Each has a distinct beginning and ending, but within the sequences themselves the movements should "not allow gaps" (Wile, 1983: 102). Pauses and gaps in technique provide openings for an attacker. And though we may realize this, when it becomes ingrained in katas, we tend not to see the connections between techniques in application—we tend not to see the techniques as combinations.

However, altering the kata's rhythm is not the same as altering the moves themselves. I am not suggesting that kata form is at all arbitrary. That would be a particularly egregious misreading. While the altering, however slight, of kata movement can lead one down a number of interesting paths, discovering all sorts of unique applications, this is not what I am suggesting. To discover the original intent of the techniques in any kata—what I would suggest is the real application—an application should adhere as closely as possible to the kata's movement. The attempt is to discover what the kata is trying to show us. In most cases, this is hidden only if we don't apply the principles.

So often we simplify things to teach them or we standardize techniques that may only be similar. Both of these are dangerous shortcuts. To investigate kata movement, we must constantly keep in mind the art's principles—principles of movement that are often shared by a broad spectrum of martial arts—and scrutinize our technique in light of these principles.

Does this mean that we should abandon the entire curriculum of training subjects, based as they are on the Gekisai katas? Not necessarily. But we should see it for what it is, separate and distinct from the classical katas—and the essence I would argue—of Goju-Ryu. They are worlds apart. The principles found within the classical katas, when applied, facilitate speed and power—in general, martial effectiveness—and those techniques and interpretations that do not conform to these principles will readily be seen to be less effective, and, in a word, questionable.

The classical Goju-Ryu katas, like Sepai, illustrate and teach these principles. The katas' patterns shows how to step off the centerline, that is, how to avoid the attacker. Second, the techniques are meant to show responses against a fully committed attacker. These are not sparring techniques. As Dan Smith notes, "*Uchinandi* [Okinawan karate] is a self-defense based solution and works best when the opponent makes the first movement of attack" (Smith, Letter 6). And last, the various classical subjects of Goju-Ryu are collections of techniques that fit together as combinations. They show variations of a finite number of themes in the same way that a classical music piece shows themes and variations. The combinations may be taken apart and put together in a variety of ways, but the first step is to see them as combinations. Each kata contains only a handful of combinations of techniques against an attacker.

For the most part, traditional Goju-Ryu practitioners have done a wonderful job investigating individual techniques, but we have been lost in this forest of technique, so to speak, unable to see the "system" for the trees. To see Goju-Ryu as a complete system, one must see the katas' techniques as combinations. And the way to see the various combinations of techniques is to apply the principles of movement to the katas. The proof, of course, will not be found in reference books but on the dojo floor.

Finally, one should remember that it is a lifetime pursuit to develop one's own self defense. It shouldn't be impossibly difficult or require great amounts of strength. If either were true, one would be least able to use it just when one needed it the most. The way I am suggesting we look at Goju-Ryu is, in a sense, more simplified. It shows Goju-Ryu as a system that makes use of certain martial principles, then gives examples to illustrate these principles, and finally shows a finite number of variations of the same principles and techniques. An understanding of this does not necessarily make the journey any shorter—one must still practice until the bones and the muscles and the blood begin to understand the technique—but the idea is to get the feet planted firmly on the right road before setting out on the journey. This is just the first step.

Matayoshi Shinpo with the
author's daughter, Phoebe.

Most nights we would walk down the hill from Matayoshi's dojo late, with the smell of mosquito coils still in the air, tired and hungry. We would walk through Heiwa Dori, feeling the soft tar on the roads, still hot from the day, looking for a late night soup shop or some place to sit and talk before turning in.

Nowadays, I find myself wishing that I had the opportunity to talk to Matayoshi one more time or wishing I had known then the right questions to ask. But Matayoshi died in 1997. I last saw him when he stayed at my house. It was another hot summer, this time in New England. My teacher, Kimo Wall, was taking Matayoshi on a driving tour of the United States, stopping to teach seminars along the way. That summer, Matayoshi had tried to explain to a friend of mine that there were really three kinds of karate. They were sitting at the dinner table. Matayoshi placed three forks on the table between them.

"Three kinds of karate," Matayoshi said, using Japanese this time. "There's what you teach to students," he said, picking up the first fork and setting it down again. "Then there's what you do for demonstrations," he said, picking up the second fork. "And then there's real karate," he said, pointing to the third fork. I think I know now what he meant. But I wish I could ask him a few more questions about real karate and how they did it in the old days.

Bibliography

Goodin, C. (1999). The 1940 karate-do special committee: The Fukyugata "promotional" kata. *Dragon Times*, 15.

Higaonna, M. (1985). *Traditional karate-do: Okinawa Goju Ryu: The fundamental techniques*. Tokyo: Japan Publications.

Johnson, N. (2000). *Barefoot Zen: The Shaolin roots of kung fu and karate*. York Beach, ME: Samuel Weiser.

Labbate, M. (2000). Developing advanced Goju-Ryu techniques. *Journal of Asian Martial Arts*, 9(1), 56–69.

Marquez, A. (1996). Okinawan journey: Legacy of the past. *Bugeisha 1*(1), 8–15.

McCarthy, P., and McCarthy, Y. (1999) *Ancient Okinawan martial arts: Koryu Uchinadi, Vol. 2*. Boston: Tuttle.

Smith, D. Letter 1—*Kata & bunkai*. Downloaded on September 22, 2001, from http://home.drenik.net/joemilos/sensei_dan_smith_letter1.htm

Smith, D. Letter 3—*Are there blocks in Okinawan kata?* Downloaded on September 22, 2001, from http://home.drenik.net/joemilos/letter_3.htm

Smith, D. Letter 6—*About tegumi*. Downloaded on September 22, 2001, from http://home.drenik.net/joemilos/letter_6.htm

Toguchi, S. (1976). *Okinawan Goju-Ryu: The fundamentals of Shoreikan karate*. Burbank, CA: Ohara Publications.

Toth, R. (2001). An analysis of parallel techniques: The kinetic connection between Sanseru and Shishochin. *Journal of Asian Martial Arts*, 10(3), 84–91.

Wile, D. (1983). *T'ai-chi touchstones: Yang family secret transmissions*. New York: Sweet Ch'i Press.

Acknowledgment

Special thanks to John Jackson, fifth dan, for his assistance in demonstrating applications for this article and for his companionship along "the martial way." Also, a special thanks to Ivan Siff, fourth dan and training partner, without whom none of this might have come to fruition. And, of course, a very special thanks to my teachers, especially Kimo Wall, who set my feet on the correct path.

index

Aragaki, Ryuko, 71
Aragaki, Seisho, 71
arm-toughening drills (koteikitai), 104
backfist (uraken), 113
Black Turtle (Genbu), 77 note 2
Blue Dragon (Seiryu), 77 note 2
breathing, 14–15, 18, 22–23, 27–28, 32–33,
    51–52, 54, 69, 71, 81–83
Bubishi, 71, 94
budo, 2, 4–5
bujutsu, 3–4
bunkai, 10, 99
Byakko, see White Tiger.
Cauley, Thomas, 7
chishi weights, 24–26
dojo, 4, 8, 11, 85, 101–102, 104, 116–119
fajing, see issuing power.
free sparring (jiu kumite), 8, 102, 118
fundamentals (kihon), 101–102
Fukyugata, 71
Funakoshi, Gichin, 9
Fuzhou, 71–72
Gekisai (I & II), 71, 101, 103, 117
Goju-Ryu, 11, 14, 28, 33, 38, 51–52, 69–72, 77, 79,
    81, 97, 99–105, 116–118
hakkei, see issuing power.
Heaven and Earth (Tenshi), 77 note 2
Higa, Seko, 98
Higaonna, Morio, 15, 72, 103
Higaonna, Kanryo (aka. Higashionna), 71–72, 77
    note 1
issuing power (Chinese fajing; Japanese
    hakkei), 30–31
Itosu, Ankoh, 102
kaho, 1–12
kakie, see push-hands.
Kakuho, 97, 100
Kanzaki, Shigekazu, 72
karate drum, 35–38, 52, 54, 61, 69, 84
kata, 1–12
Kingai-Ryu, 97, 100
Kinjo, Hiroshi, 71
knife-hand (shuto), 38, 53, 56–57, 62–64, 67,
    87, 91, 94, 107
kobudo, 97
Kodokan, 4
Kojo, Taitei, 71
Kururunfa, 71, 104
Kyoda, Juhatsu, 71–72

Kyokushinkai, 4
Masanobu, Shinjo, 102
Matayoshi, Shinpo, 97–100, 103, 119
Miyagi, Chojun, 14, 29, 52, 71–72,
    77 note 2, 101, 103
Miyazato, Ei'ichi, 99
Motobo-ryu, 2
Nagamine, Shoshin, 71
Naha, 71, 77 note 1, 98
Nahate, 71
Nakaima, Kenri, 77
palm strike, 38, 40–41, 53–54, 57–61, 63–65,
    67, 72, 87
push-hands (kakie), 52, 56–60, 67, 69
Red Sparrow (Shujakku), 77 note 2
ryu ("streams"), 4
Ryu Ryu Ko (aka. Ru Ru Ko), 71
Saifa, 11, 71, 104
Sakiyama, Kitoku, 77
Sanchin, 14–16, 18, 20–23, 26–30, 32, 52–55,
    61–65, 67, 69, 71, 82, 84, 104
sanchin stance, 15–16, 18, 20–21, 23, 28, 53–54,
    61, 72
Sanseru, 70–77
Sepai, 71, 104–106, 117–118
Sesan, 71, 104
Seiunchin, 71, 79–83, 85–86, 104
Shishochin, 70–77
Shorin-Ryu, 102
Shorinji-Ryu, 7
Shotokan, 4
spear-hand, 72, 80
sticking (muchimi), 39, 41–42, 56, 59–60, 103,
    107
Suparimpei, 71, 104
taisabaki (body movement), 43, 103
tanden, 15, 22–24, 27–28, 31, 62, 84
Tenshi (Heaven and Earth), 77 note 2
Tensho, 52–69, 71, 77 note 2
Toguchi, Seikichi, 103
transitioning, 52–54, 61–65, 67–69, 82–83
Udun-di, 2
Uehara, Seikichi, 2
vital point striking (kyushojutsu), 79, 86, 95,
    104
Wall, Kimo, 98, 119–120
White Tiger (byakko), 77 note 2
World War II, 5, 102
Yagi Meitoku, 77 note 2

Made in the USA
San Bernardino, CA
23 November 2015